MEANINGFUL AND MANAGEABLE
PROGRAM ASSESSMENT

MEANINGFUL AND MANAGEABLE PROGRAM ASSESSMENT

A How-To Guide for Higher Education Faculty

Laura J. Massa and Margaret Kasimatis

STERLING, VIRGINIA

COPYRIGHT © 2017 BY
STYLUS PUBLISHING, LLC.

Published by Stylus Publishing, LLC.
22883 Quicksilver Drive
Sterling, Virginia 20166-2102

Library of Congress Cataloging-in-Publication Data

Names: Massa, Laura J., author. |
Kasimatis, Margaret, author.
Title: Meaningful and manageable program assessment : a how-to
guide for higher education faculty/Laura J. Massa and Margaret
Kasimatis.
Description: Sterling, Virginia : Stylus Publishing, 2017. |
Includes bibliographical references and index.
Identifiers: LCCN 2017009837 (print) |
LCCN 2017031730 (ebook) |
ISBN 9781620365656 (uPDF) |
ISBN 9781620365663 (ePub, mobi) |
ISBN 9781620365632 (cloth : alk. paper) |
ISBN 9781620365649 (pbk. : alk. paper) |
ISBN 9781620365656 (library networkable e-edition) |
ISBN 9781620365663 (consumer e-edition)
Subjects: LCSH: Universities and colleges--United States--
Evaluation--Handbooks, manuals, etc. |
Education, Higher--United States--Evaluation--
Handbooks, manuals, etc. |
Educational evaluation--United States--Handbooks, manuals, etc.
Classification: LCC LB2331.63 (ebook) |
LCC LB2331.63 .M38 2017 (print) |
DDC 378.00973--dc23
LC record available at https://lccn.loc.gov/2017009837

13-digit ISBN: 978-1-62036-563-2 (cloth)
13-digit ISBN: 978-1-62036-564-9 (paperback)
13-digit ISBN: 978-1-62036-565-6 (library networkable e-edition)
13-digit ISBN: 978-1-62036-566-3 (consumer e-edition)

Printed in the United States of America

All first editions printed on acid-free paper
that meets the American National Standards Institute
Z39-48 Standard.

Bulk Purchases

Quantity discounts are available for use in workshops and for
staff development.
Call 1-800-232-0223

First Edition, 2017

We dedicate this book to faculty, staff, and administrators who are committed to understanding and improving the learning of your students. You are our inspiration.

Contents

INTRODUCTION

Putting Assessment Into Context

Over the last few years, institutions of higher education have been experiencing increased pressure to provide evidence of student learning. It's no longer sufficient to say that our students complete the required courses, graduate, and get jobs. Don't get us wrong—these things will always be necessary for an institution to be considered successfully functioning. What we are saying is that the outside world now demands more. In other words, assessment of student learning has become essential.

External demands that colleges and universities engage in assessment of student learning have been around since the mid-1980s; however, these demands for accountability have intensified more recently as public concern about high costs, high student debt loads, and low completion rates have led to questions about whether college is worth it. Publications such as *Academically Adrift* (Arum & Roska, 2011), *Our Underachieving Colleges* (Bok, 2006), and the report from the Spellings Commission (U.S. Department of Education, 2006) have also led to questions about what students really gain from a college education. These public concerns have translated into requirements that institutions not only engage in assessment but also provide evidence of what students have learned as a result of their education.

At the same time, regional accreditors have a goal of fostering continuous improvement and, as a result, they are increasingly demanding to know how institutions are using information about student learning to guide institutional improvement. For example, the WASC Senior College and University Commission (2013) has the following as part of its criteria for review statements: "Assessment of teaching, learning, and the campus environment . . . is undertaken, used for improvement, and incorporated into institutional planning processes" and "Faculty and other educators take responsibility for evaluating the effectiveness of teaching and learning processes. . . . The findings from such inquiries are applied to the design and improvement of curricula, pedagogy, and assessment methodology" (p. 21).

In addition, institutions are operating with increasingly constrained resources in a rapidly changing, increasingly competitive environment. In an effort to gain a competitive edge in this environment without breaking the bank, institutions are turning to strategic planning and prioritization processes, as well as marketing campaigns, that focus on academic quality. All of these processes can benefit from (and ideally should involve) evidence of what students gain from their college experience.

All of these pressures have resulted in increased assessment activity on most college and university campuses. Yet, those who are responsible for leading assessment often need clear instruction for how to go about the work. They need guidance on how to measure student learning, how to engage their faculty colleagues in the work, and how to ensure that assessment results are actually used for improvement. Once they get it going, they need advice on how to ensure the sustainability of their assessment work.

While all of us share the need to engage in sustainable, meaningful assessment, it is important to keep in mind that assessment work is carried out within individual institutional contexts. Each institution is at a different stage of development in terms of assessing student learning, and each has its own mission, culture, organizational structure, and educational focus, all of which have implications for how you approach assessment of student learning in your program.

The Purpose of This Book

This book provides faculty, current academic leaders, and aspiring academic leaders with the information they need to design and carry out successful program assessment plans within their unique institutional context. It provides a straightforward overview of assessment concepts and principles, as well as practical, easy-to-follow instructions for multiple assessment measurement tools and key steps in the assessment process. In other words, we view this book as a handy, all-in-one, how-to guide. In this respect, we believe it will be particularly helpful to faculty members who are charged with leading assessment efforts in their respective departments. For example, the chair of a program assessment committee might take this book to meetings and use it as a guide to help the committee work through the practical steps of getting program assessment done.

In addition, the text guides readers toward the development of a culture of assessment. For example, it includes tips for making the assessment process meaningful, suggestions for how academic administrators can recognize and support faculty assessment work, and strategies for embedding assessment into ongoing institutional processes. The development of such a culture, one in which internal interests drive assessment activity, will help institutions to meet today's external demands with ease and be well prepared for the next evolution in external assessment requirements.

Everything presented in this guidebook has been developed by the authors in our work as assessment leaders on college and university campuses. As the director of assessment at Loyola Marymount University (LMU) for nine years, Laura has provided consulting support, workshops, and other resources to increase faculty capacity to engage in meaningful assessment. She has seen firsthand how the approaches described in this guide have made a positive difference for faculty and academic programs, for example, when the assessment process leads to faculty conversations about what is really happening in their curriculum and how they can use that information to improve their work as educators. Margaret has more than 14 years of experience in academic administration with an additional 10 years of experience as a full-time faculty member. As such, she has served in several different roles that have informed her approach to assessment. In her current role in the provost's office at LMU she was the architect of the recent strategic planning process and led the campus through a very successful reaccreditation process. Through these and other experiences she has witnessed the importance of institutional context; leadership; and developing structures, processes, and resources in creating a culture of assessment and improvement.

The text is inspired by and filled with tips and examples from our work. We have tried to capture the conversational tone that has helped us to successfully teach assessment principles and practices to faculty and administrators from a variety of academic disciplines and institutions. We hope that when reading this guide you feel as if a friendly, supportive assessment professional is by your side.

In short, the goal of this guide is to provide readers with a straightforward approach to doing assessment in a way that is meaningful, manageable, and sustainable over time.

Organization of This Book

This guide begins with an overview of the assessment process, as well as key assessment concepts and principles. Subsequent modules provide detailed instructions and specific tips for carrying out each step of the process, including three modules focused on creating and implementing specific assessment measurement tools. In the final module we compile all of the tips we provided throughout the book—tips that we hope will help you to avoid common assessment pitfalls and ensure your assessment efforts are successful.

We recommend that you begin by reading module 1, "An Overview of Assessment Concepts and Principles: Improving Student Learning," which provides a framework that will enhance your understanding of each of the steps of the process that are spelled out in detail in subsequent modules.

However, after that, each of the modules is designed to stand alone. You do not need to read the modules in order, nor do you need to read all of them, to benefit from their guidance. For example, your program may already have a good list of student learning outcomes, so you might want to jump straight to the module about how to construct and use curriculum and outcome maps (module 4, "Curriculum and Outcome Mapping: Understanding the Path to Student Learning in Your Program"). Or, perhaps you have already collected some assessment data but you're not sure how to interpret the results and use them for improvement. In that case you might want to start by reading about how to summarize and present your evidence (module 10, "Organizing, Summarizing, and Presenting Your Evidence: Using Microsoft Excel to Make Sense of Your Data") or you might even want to jump ahead and start by reading about how to interpret and use your findings (module 11, "Closing the Loop: Interpreting Results and Taking Action"). Wherever you go next, you'll find that each module includes references to modules on related topics. That way, if you find you need additional guidance on something, you'll know where to look for it. Above all else, we hope that you find this book helpful in developing meaningful, manageable, and sustainable assessment of student learning in your program.

I

AN OVERVIEW OF ASSESSMENT CONCEPTS AND PRINCIPLES

Improving Student Learning

I f you've ever taught a course, then you've likely engaged in a less formal version of the assessment processes that are presented in this guidebook. For example, you may have had the experience of testing students on a topic that you thought you had covered clearly, only to find that students could not answer questions about it correctly. As a result, you went back over the topic in class in an effort to make sure that students got it. In other words, you had something you wanted students to learn; you understood how they were supposed to learn it; you checked to see if they had actually learned it; and then, when they didn't learn it to your satisfaction, you took action to improve their learning. This is *assessment*.

In this module we provide an overview of the more formal assessment process that programs follow to understand achievement of program student learning outcomes, including important concepts and principles. Our goal is to provide a framework that will help you to understand each of the steps in the process—steps that are spelled out in detail in subsequent modules.

Defining *Assessment*

One of the most challenging aspects of trying to help people understand and conduct meaningful and manageable assessment is the fact that the word *assessment* can mean many different things, depending on the context. For example, it can be used to connote a valuation, a judgment, an opinion, or an evaluation. In specific professional settings, it carries still more meanings.

Even within an educational setting, *assessment* can mean measurement, grading, or a process. With all of these possible definitions there is often an understandable level of confusion, or even fear, about what assessment really means. One such fear that we've encountered many times is the fear that assessment is really a way to evaluate the performance of individual faculty. Let us reassure you that is not what assessment of student learning in your program is about.

From our perspective, *assessment* is defined as a systematic process for understanding and improving student learning (Angelo, 1995). This is a relatively short definition, but it contains several important concepts:

- **Systematic process:** Use of this phrase is intended to imply that assessment is not an ad hoc or onetime event. Rather, it should be built into the ongoing work of the program.
- **Understanding:** We use this word instead of *measure* to imply that assessment involves efforts to get a clear picture not only of what and how much students know and are able to do but also how they have learned or why they haven't.
- **Improving:** This word conveys that assessment does not stop after evidence of student learning has been collected. Instead, the reason for gathering the evidence—for understanding what, how much, and how students have learned—is to use the results to improve student learning.
- **Student learning:** This is what it's all about. It's the reason we teach. It's why we have colleges and universities. If we care about learning, then we should care about assessment.

Levels of Assessment

Within a higher education setting, assessment of student learning can take place at multiple levels, including student, course, program, and institution.

- **Individual student:** Uses the individual student, and his or her learning, as the level of analysis. It answers the question, What has this student learned?
- **Course:** Uses aggregate student learning results in an individual course as the level of analysis. It answers the question, What have students learned as a result of their experiences in this specific course?
- **Program:** Uses the academic program as the level of analysis. It answers the question, What have students learned as a result of their experiences in your program's curriculum?

- **Institution:** Uses the institution as the level of analysis. It answers the question, What have students learned as a result of their entire experience at your institution?

In this book our focus is on program-level assessment, although many of the principles and techniques we describe can also be applied to assessment at the course or institution level. We should note, however, that you can't sum up all the assessments at one level to get a complete picture of whether you're achieving outcomes at another level. For example, it would not be appropriate to conduct course-level assessment in each of the required courses in a major and use those results as indicators of whether program-level student learning outcomes are being achieved. This is because course outcomes and program outcomes, while related, have different foci. Moreover, although most assessment measurement tools can be employed at multiple levels, there are important qualitative differences in how they are used at the various levels. For example, at the individual-student level, a rubric is used to determine a student's grade on an assignment by summing up all of the component scores, whereas at the program level each component of a rubric is aggregated across students in order to understand accomplishment of that particular learning outcome component.

The Assessment Process

Because assessment is a systematic process, not an isolated task, there are multiple steps involved. The following is an illustration of what this process looks like when it occurs in a perfect world (see Figure 1.1). You'll notice that it has a fluid, cyclical pattern that, once entered, goes around and around. In reality, this process often gets disrupted and steps are performed out of order—something we go into in more detail a bit later—but before we get into that, we think it's important that you understand what this process looks like under ideal circumstances. Let's walk through the process illustrated in Figure 1.1.

Step 1: Articulate Mission and Goals

The assessment process begins with an articulation of the program's mission and goals. As discussed in module 2, "Mission, Goals, and Outcomes: Looking at the Big Picture," a mission statement explains why your program exists and what it hopes to achieve. Another way of thinking about a mission statement is that it succinctly describes the essential nature of your program. Viewed this way, it becomes clear why you need to start here, because the essential nature of your program will impact what goals you are trying to accomplish.

Figure 1.1. The assessment process.

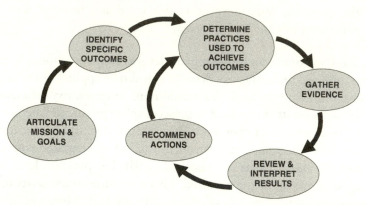

Learning goals are drawn from the mission statement and are broad statements that describe the essential learning—knowledge, skills, attitudes, and values—that graduates of your program should accomplish. Your learning goals are the link between your global mission and the very specific and measurable statements of expected learning expressed by your learning outcomes. Learning goals, while more specific than the expectations for learning expressed by your mission statement, are not written in such a way that they are measurable. In fact, they are generally so broad as to allow multiple learning outcomes to be drawn from each learning goal.

Step 2: Identify Specific Outcomes

Student learning outcomes are statements that specify what students will know, be able to do, or value when they complete a program. They are drawn from the program's learning goals. For example, if you have a learning goal that states your students will demonstrate professional communication skills, then you will most likely want to write learning outcomes for both written and oral communication skills. Similarly, if you have a learning goal related to conducting research in the social sciences, you would have several learning outcomes for specific skills related to social science research. In the latter example, the goal would be phrased something like, "Graduates of our program will possess the skills necessary to conduct research in the social sciences." A learning outcome related to this goal might be, "Graduates of the program will be able to design appropriate measures of the variables in a study."

In module 3, "Student Learning Outcomes: Articulating What You Want Students to Learn," we provide detailed guidance for how to write a student learning outcome statement. It is important to note that learning outcome statements express the things that students will take away from your program, or, as we like to say, they note the things your students will walk out with. Learning outcome statements do not describe what faculty will provide or how happy students will be with your program; they describe the results of students' learning experiences in your program. Outcomes indicate learning that is observable, or measurable. This does not mean that your learning outcomes have to be objectively quantifiable, but it does mean that they can be measured in some way.

Step 3: Determine Practices Used to Achieve Outcomes

As described earlier in this module, assessment involves not only measuring what students have learned but also understanding *how* students have learned. Thus, spelling out the ways the program tries to foster the desired learning— that is, the context in which the learning takes place—is very important.

In module 4, "Curriculum and Outcome Mapping: Understanding the Path to Student Learning in Your Program," we describe in detail how to create curriculum maps and outcome maps. These tools depict the alignment between a program's curriculum and the learning outcomes of the program; that is, they show you where in the curriculum each outcome is addressed and provide information about how it is addressed.

Curriculum maps and outcome maps are valuable tools that can serve a couple of purposes in the assessment process. First, a curriculum map can serve as a preliminary assessment that helps you identify "gaps" in your curriculum. For example, if a curriculum map shows that one of your program's student learning outcomes is not addressed in any of the required courses in the major, then you know immediately that changes need to be made. Second, detailed curriculum maps and outcome maps can be very helpful in determining when and how to collect evidence of student achievement of a learning outcome. For example, if your curriculum map shows that the only course that all seniors take that involves a significant writing assignment is the senior seminar in the major, then you know that gathering the papers from that course would provide the best available evidence of learning for the assessment of your program's learning outcome related to written communication. We will discuss these and other uses and benefits of curriculum maps and outcome maps in more detail in module 4. In module 5, "Planning: Creating a Meaningful and Manageable Assessment Plan for Your Program," we will show you how your map is an essential component of your program's assessment plan.

Step 4: Gather Evidence

This is the step that most people envision when they think of assessment, namely, collecting data. We prefer to call it gathering evidence for two reasons. First, the word *data* tends to imply quantitative methods and that can be off-putting to many faculty. It is also the case that sometimes assessments are qualitative. Second, we use the word *evidence* to emphasize that whatever information is gathered should be meaningful in terms of helping faculty understand student learning in their program. Another way to say it is that *data* simply means information, whereas *evidence* means information that can help you draw a conclusion.

In module 6, "Assessment Measurement Tools: Determining What Your Students Are Learning," we provide an overview of different types of assessment measurement tools. That module is followed by detailed guidance on how to construct and use three essential assessment measurement tools: rubrics (module 7), exams (module 8), and surveys (module 9). Here we offer a few important principles to keep in mind when gathering evidence of student learning.

First, as much as possible, you should use direct evidence of student learning. As the name implies, this type of measurement involves direct observation of student performance. Examples of such measures include exam items and rubric evaluation of student work or performances. Second, it is important that your measures are tied to your learning outcomes and learning context. For example, an external, standardized exam may not be appropriate to use if it does not provide you with information about student accomplishment of the learning outcomes for your program.

Step 5: Review and Interpret Results

This is the step where you make sense out of the evidence you've collected; that is, you decide what it's telling you about what, how much, and how students are learning in your program. This is also the step where many people get stuck. They have the evidence but they don't know how to interpret it.

In module 10, "Organizing, Summarizing, and Presenting Your Evidence: Using Microsoft Excel to Make Sense of Your Data," we provide some tips for organizing and analyzing quantitative data, and in module 11, "Closing the Loop: Interpreting Results and Taking Action," we guide you through the process of understanding what your assessment evidence means in a way that will help you use it to improve student learning in your program.

Step 6: Recommend Actions

Once you've developed a clear interpretation of your assessment results, you are in a position to "close the loop"; that is, make and carry out recommendations for actions that will improve learning in your program. These could range from clarifying the language of your learning outcomes to revising your curriculum. When you carry out actions for improvement, you modify the practices used to achieve the outcome, thus bringing you back to the top of the cycle (i.e., closing the loop).

In the module on closing the loop (module 11) we describe some of the different types of actions that might be appropriate based on the pattern of results you observe. We also provide helpful tips that will increase the likelihood that your recommendations are implemented and can be evaluated in subsequent assessment cycles. In module 12, "Record Keeping: Keeping Track of Your Work," we share approaches to keeping a record of the entire process you've just completed, including the changes you made to close the loop. This record will serve many purposes, including helping you to understand the impact of the changes you made the next time you assess the learning outcome.

A Word About Assessment in the Real World

As noted earlier, the steps just described represent an ideal version of the assessment process. However, we live in the real world, and reality can be messy. For example, it is possible that when you construct your curriculum map you see a pattern that suggests that changes should be made in your curriculum before you've even gathered any evidence. Or you might have been collecting evidence of student learning all along and realize that you should start by aligning that evidence to your program's student learning outcomes and then reflecting on what it tells you about each of those outcomes. Throughout this book we will provide tips for addressing some of these issues and using assessment for improving student learning whether you followed the "ideal" process or not. Ultimately, no matter where you enter the assessment process or what disruptions prevent you from following the ideal pattern, your goal should be to keep working toward carrying out the steps that will help you to understand and improve student learning in your program.

Addressing Workload Issues and Building a Culture of Assessment

Despite the best efforts of faculty and administrators, the assessment process can stall and fail to lead to the desired understanding and improvement of student learning. Too often we've seen a group of program faculty work hard to gather evidence of student learning, but because of competing priorities in the program there is never time to discuss how to act on the results during a faculty meeting. We've also seen programs that have an assessment champion who leads them through meaningful assessment processes for a year or two, but then that person goes on sabbatical and efforts wane. The result in both situations tends to be a confirmation of negative perceptions of assessment, namely, that assessment is a lot of work that is not meaningful or helpful.

This book is designed to help you avoid some of the mistakes that can lead to inaction or assessment burnout. In particular, module 13, "Creating a Culture of Assessment: Tips for Keeping Assessment Meaningful, Manageable, and Sustainable," provides helpful tips for addressing workload issues, strategies for ensuring that the assessment process is meaningful, and suggestions for how to embed assessment into the ongoing work of the program.

Summary

Assessment is a systematic process for understanding and improving student learning. It begins with an articulation of a program's mission, goals, and learning outcomes and involves determining the practices used to achieve the learning outcomes, gathering evidence of student learning, interpreting the results, and making recommendations for changes that will improve student learning. It is not always possible to follow the ideal process, but you should not let a fear of imperfection get in the way of moving forward with efforts to understand and improve student learning. While engaging in assessment, it is also important to employ strategies to keep the process meaningful and manageable in order to create a sustainable culture of assessment.

MISSION, GOALS, AND OUTCOMES

Looking at the Big Picture

The essential purpose of every institution of higher education is to educate students. You'll certainly find this described in your institution's mission statement. What you'll also notice about your institution's mission statement is that it is probably not written in such a way that you can easily capture how well you are achieving your mission to educate students. That's why we get more descriptive with learning goal statements and much more specific about expected learning with learning outcome statements. When we work to understand and improve student learning outcomes, we are indirectly working to understand and improve achievement of our mission. In this module we'll check out the big picture and look at how student learning outcomes, student learning goals, and mission statements all connect and clarify how assessment of your program's student learning outcomes helps us to understand mission accomplishment.

Mission Statement

A mission statement explains why your institution exists and what it hopes to achieve. It articulates your institution's essential nature, its values, and its work. Every institution should have a mission statement that guides the work of the institution. Individual units within an institution, like your program, do not necessarily have their own mission statements. After all, your work can be said to be driven by the institution's mission; however, we believe it can be helpful to have a program mission statement to guide your work. A program mission statement can certainly be helpful for assessment, and it can be useful in thinking about long-term planning for your program, as well as serve as a guide during formal academic program review processes.

Writing a mission statement does not have to be a complicated, long-term project. You can draft an initial mission statement in a meeting, with edits to follow. Those edits can be completed in additional meetings or even electronically, such as through a shared cloud file or via e-mail. It can help to approach the task of writing a mission statement for your program as something that does not have to be immediately perfect. Mission statements often take time to fully form, typically evolving as you learn from assessment, program review, and other information gathering and analysis projects that you undertake. Your initial goal should be to get something down that you feel like you can work with and that captures each of the key elements.

Your program's mission statement does not need to be long; typically, mission statements are only about a paragraph in length. The three key elements that are commonly included in a mission statement are:

1. **Why do you exist?** This is essentially a statement of purpose. It tells the reader why you do what you do. You should note any values or principles that drive your work, such as those of your discipline and those of your institution. Generally, it is good practice to consider how the work of your program contributes to the achievement of the institution's mission.
2. **What do you do?** Provide a summary of your essential work. Typically this will include an expression of what students will learn from your curriculum. Be sure to note any distinctive features of your program.
3. **Who is served by your program?** These are your stakeholders. Typically these include your students and faculty but can also include staff and external constituents you serve.

As with writing just about anything, it can help to do a bit of research before you begin. We recommend looking at the mission statements of programs that are similar to yours at other institutions, as well as mission statements from a variety of programs across your institution. This will help give you a sense of what is typical for your discipline and your institution. To get you started, we've included a handful of examples of program mission statements from institutions across the country in Figure 2.1.

Student Learning Goals

Within your mission statement you've indicated something about what students will learn from the program; however, in that brief paragraph you have likely indicated something very general. Student learning goals are drawn from the mission statement to indicate the knowledge, skills, attitudes, and values expected in graduates of your program. Your learning goals are the link

Figure 2.1. Examples of program mission statements.

Art Department, Augsburg College (2016)

The Art Department's mission is to consistently give students a sound basis for visual literacy and appreciation, accomplishment in art making, and an understanding of historical context, and provide opportunities for community engagement and visibility. Through experiential learning and critical engagement, we foster understanding of and respect for the crucial contributions of art to society.

The Art Department values and encourages scholarship that supports and expands discipline-specific knowledge and skills necessary for creative production, critical engagement in the life of the discipline, instruction of the highest quality, and integration of the institutional mission with cultural and social issues. We honor and encourage varied, experimental, and integrative approaches to this work, especially that which

- arises from and/or feeds back into classroom activities;
- encourages collaboration with peers, students and community;
- involves faculty and professionals in the art world, which reflects the highest standards of the profession and discipline as recognized by experts and peers in the field and;
- fosters commitment to diversity.

History Department, Tulane University (n.d.)

The history department's mission for our majors is to ground students in the foundations of the human experience. We explore cause-and-effect relationships in human affairs, and encourage them to understand the power and complexity of the past in shaping the contemporary human condition. We strive to convey to all our students an understanding of historical actors, events, belief systems, material realities, and cultural values that have shaped the world in which they live. History courses at both the introductory and advanced levels emphasize focus and in-depth historical knowledge and skills that are essential for personal and professional growth and success—including critical analysis and reasoning and written and oral communication. In so doing, our mission helps fulfill Tulane University's mission to enrich the capacity of its students to think, to learn, and to act and lead with integrity and wisdom.

Mathematics Department, Southern Oregon University (2005)

The Mathematics Department at Southern Oregon University is committed to providing an excellent major for students whose career goals are K–12 teaching, immediate entry into the workforce, or pursuit of a graduate degree in mathematics. The department is an active partner with our region and with other programs in science, social science, business, and education by providing specialized mathematical training or expertise.

(Continues)

FIGURE 2.1. (*Continued*)

The department is committed to high quality instruction for all students in mathematics courses, and it nurtures pleasant and constructive faculty-student interaction.

Psychology Department, University of North Carolina Wilmington (2013)

The Department of Psychology supports the UNCW and CAS missions by advancing the scientific discipline of psychology through the synergistic relationship between teaching, research, and service. We are dedicated to excellence in our primary purpose—preparing students to become psychologically literate citizens with the skills necessary to flourish and engage in life activities that serve to advance scientific knowledge, solve problems, and actively engage in efforts to improve our communities and beyond. We accomplish this purpose by utilizing best practices in science education, close instructional contact and research training with experts in a variety of fields of psychology, conducting and disseminating cutting-edge scientific research, and fostering engagement in applied learning/service opportunities that connect students with the larger community beyond the classroom.

between your global mission and the very specific and measurable statements of expected learning expressed by your student learning outcomes.

Student learning goals are broad statements that describe essential learning that graduates of your program should accomplish. These statements, while more specific than the expectations for learning expressed by your mission statement, are not written in such a way that they are measurable. In fact, they are generally broad and allow multiple learning outcomes to be drawn from each learning goal. For example, let's say your mission statement expresses that you prepare students for their careers. This could lead to a number of learning goals, including one about communication skills, such as "Graduates of our program will possess the communication skills necessary for professional success." The communication skills that you want your students to achieve likely include a number of rich and complex things; things that would be a challenge to measure in the holistic way that is expressed by your learning goal. To measure achievement of this goal, you would need to specify learning outcomes for the required communication skills, likely written communication, oral communication, and possibly more that are relevant to your specific discipline. In this way, learning goals serve as a bridge between your mission statement and your student learning outcomes.

In Table 2.1 we've provided a few examples of how programs at different institutions use student learning goal statements as a bridge between their mission and their student learning outcomes. For example, in the department of biology at Bates College (n.d.), the mission stresses the importance

TABLE 2.1

Examples of Program Mission Statements

Biology, Bates College (n.d.)	
From the mission statement	We prepare students for future careers in the life sciences, to understand biological issues, and to use scientific thinking in their future lives. We offer classes and laboratory sessions that include inquiry-based studies, and we emphasize scientific thought, not just the acquisition of information.
One of the program goals drawn from this mission	Biology majors will explore connections between biological science and society.
Some of the outcomes drawn from this goal	Students will apply scientific thinking to everyday problems.
	Students will articulate the relevance of biology to society.

Business Program, Creighton University (n.d.)	
From the mission statement	Guided by our Jesuit heritage, we form leaders who use their business education to promote justice and improve the world.
One of the program goals drawn from this mission	Creighton-formed business leaders will commit to action that demonstrates care for others.
Some of the outcomes drawn from this goal	Students will analyze a business ethics situation and propose a course of action.
	Students will demonstrate knowledge of strategies to work effectively with others regardless of race, ethnicity, culture, gender, religion, and sexual orientation.

Department of Theatre and Communication Arts, Linfield College (n.d.)	
From the mission statement	The programs in the Department of Theatre and Communication Arts seek to connect learning, life, and community by exploring the interaction of persons and institutions through symbolic messages. Whether expressed creatively from the theatrical stage, rhetorically from the speaker's platform, or interpersonally within social relationships, appreciating and reflecting upon these messages are essential to an understanding of a diverse society and ourselves.

(Continues)

TABLE 2.1 (*Continued*)

One of the program goals drawn from this mission	Students will acquire the skills necessary to function as mindful, creative, and responsible individuals who appreciate the diversity and ambiguity of theatrical experiences and the role of theatre in society.
Some of the outcomes drawn from this goal	Students will think conceptually about and critically evaluate text, performance, and production.
	Students will explain production processes, aesthetic properties of style, and the way these shape and are shaped by artistic and cultural forces.

Note. Student learning goal statements are drawn from the mission, and measurable student learning outcome statements are drawn from the goals.

of students developing scientific thinking skills and utilizing those skills both while students and in the future. A goal drawn from this mission expresses that students will explore connections between the science they have studied and society. From this goal, multiple student learning outcomes have been drawn, including one that expresses that students will apply scientific thinking to everyday problems.

When you write your student learning goals, three basic components should be included in each.

1. Who is doing the learning. Typically this is written as *students* or *graduates of the program* but can be customized for your program as you like. For example, you might want to begin your goals with something like, "Students earning a degree in art history."
2. A description of the nature of that learning, such as *possess, demonstrate,* or *understand.*
3. The learning to be achieved, such as *communication skills necessary for professional success* or *research skills needed to be successful lifelong learners.*

That last component of each of your student learning goals—the learning to be achieved—is the part that takes the most reflection and work to develop.

The primary source for the list of things your students should learn is your mission statement. A good approach for developing this list is to take the parts of your mission that speak to student learning and break each down into those things students should know, be able to do, and value. For example, if your mission statement expresses, "Students will make informed decisions that positively impact the world," then you might have goals expressing the need to think critically and to follow disciplinary ethical guidelines. Or, if your mission statement says you prepare students for their careers, this could lead to a goal about communication skills, but also goals about knowledge of your discipline's major subject matter and primary methodological approaches, valuing lifelong learning, and more.

Ideally, you will work with colleagues in your program to develop the list of essential learning to be achieved through completing your program. Each of you will bring your own perspective to the conversation, resulting in a richer set of student learning goals. To broaden your perspectives, it can help to review the learning goals of programs like yours at other institutions, as well as the learning goals of other programs at your own institution. We also find it can be helpful to check with your disciplinary organization to see if they provide a suggested list of learning goals for graduates at various degree levels. These kinds of lists can help you to make sure you are capturing widely agreed-upon essential learning for your discipline.

Before we leave learning goals, it is important to note that there is no rule or magic number that dictates how many student learning goals your program should have. The number of learning goals you have should be reflective of those essential learning components that are expressed by your mission. We have worked with programs that have successfully captured that essential learning in as little as a single very broad learning goal, as well as upward of 10 learning goals, and everything in between. When deciding how many learning goals to have, it is important to keep in mind that each goal will lead to one or more student learning outcomes that must be assessed. It is also important to keep your learning goals focused on essential learning. This focus will help to make sure that each goal is meaningful and will lead toward a more manageable assessment plan.

Student Learning Outcomes

Program student learning outcomes are clear, concise statements that describe how students can demonstrate their mastery of program student learning goals. There are usually multiple learning outcomes for each goal. Outcomes are more specific than goals and are intentionally written in a way that allows you to measure achievement of each outcome. That ability to be measured is essential for understanding how well we are achieving our goals and, ultimately, understanding how well we are achieving our mission.

Earlier we looked at an example statement of learning expectations from a mission statement that indicated that the program prepares students for careers in the field. From this we drew a goal about communication skills, and from this goal we can draw multiple student learning outcomes. For example, we might have a written communication learning outcome stating, "Students will effectively communicate information in writing that follows disciplinary conventions." We would also have an oral communication outcome such as, "Students will deliver effective oral presentations to communicate ideas and scholarly findings." These learning outcomes are expressed in a way that allows us to assess student achievement of them.

The next module provides instruction for developing well-written learning outcomes that specify how students can demonstrate their mastery of your program's learning goals. Writing your student learning outcomes is a key first step in understanding your curriculum through mapping (see module 4, "Curriculum and Outcome Mapping: Understanding the Path to Student Learning in Your Program"), planning your program's assessment (see module 5, "Planning: Creating a Meaningful and Manageable Assessment Plan for Your Program"), and carrying out that plan as described throughout the book.

The Big Picture

Let's take a step back and look at how these three elements—mission statement, student learning goals, and student learning outcomes—all connect. As a program, you will have one mission statement. Your mission statement will provide a global perspective on the learning you want graduates of your program to achieve. From your mission statement, you will draw multiple descriptive learning goals. These goals will describe the learning that is essential for graduates of your program to achieve. From each of your learning goals, you will draw multiple student learning outcome statements. These outcome statements will specifically indicate how students can demonstrate their achievement of the program goals. It helps us to think of these three elements as having a tree-like structure, like that shown in Figure 2.2.

Figure 2.2. The connection between your program's mission statement, student learning goals, and student learning outcomes.

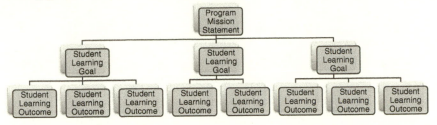

Note. Your program's mission statement provides a general description of expectations for learning. From this, multiple student learning goals are drawn to indicate the knowledge, skills, attitudes, and values expected in graduates of your program. Your learning goals are the link between your global mission and the very specific and measurable statements of expected learning expressed by your student learning outcomes. Multiple student learning outcomes are typically drawn from each learning goal.

Summary

The assessment process focuses on understanding and improving student learning outcomes, which are at the base of the structure shown in Figure 2.2. Assessment is an important process that helps us to continually improve our work as educators. What's important to understand about this process is that when we work to improve learning outcomes, we are really working toward our learning goals and, ultimately, toward achieving our mission.

3

STUDENT LEARNING OUTCOMES

Articulating What You Want Students to Learn

As we learned in module 2, student learning outcomes specify how students will demonstrate the knowledge, skills, and values that are suggested by your mission statement and described in your student learning goals. In this module we will look at why we need to get this specific, break down the elements of a learning outcome, and provide an approach to writing meaningful and measurable outcomes.

Why Do We Need Student Learning Outcomes?

One reason we need student learning outcomes is that they are essential for understanding and improving student learning. Because outcomes specify the knowledge and skills we expect students to learn and how we expect them to demonstrate that learning, they allow us to develop assessment measurement tools that tell us specifically what students have successfully learned and what could use improvement.

In addition, the process of specifying learning outcomes for your program helps you and your faculty colleagues to develop a shared understanding of what students are supposed to accomplish. The shared understanding allows you to structure a coherent curriculum that fosters students' knowledge and skills in key areas, as well as to plan and revise courses in a way that meaningfully contributes to the big picture of what students are supposed to gain.

Finally, students benefit when outcomes are clearly communicated to them, such as on the program's website or in course syllabi. Publishing learning outcomes can be a first step in engaging students in conversation about the outcomes, which helps students to better understand what they are supposed to learn. Clarity about what they are supposed to learn may motivate students to work harder (Davis, 2009; Winkelmes, 2013; Winkelmes et al., 2016) and help them reflect on what they've learned and how they've gone about learning it, essentially helping students to develop metacognition skills that are important for lifelong learning.

What Is a Student Learning Outcome?

Student learning outcomes are statements that specify what students will know, be able to do, or value when they complete a program. As we discussed previously, each student learning outcome is directly drawn from the program's learning goals. For example, if you have a learning goal that states your students will demonstrate professional communication skills, then you will most likely want to write student learning outcomes for both written and spoken communication skills.

A student learning outcome consists of three elements:

1. An *opening phrase* to indicate who will demonstrate the learning
   a. Typical opening phrases include "Students will" or "Graduates of the program will."
   b. These phrases can also be customized to your program, for example, "Computer science majors will" or "Graduates of the athletic training program will."
2. An *action word* that clearly describes the behavior to be observed
   a. The action word indicates *how* the student will demonstrate his or her learning and is typically an indicator of the level of learning the student is expected to achieve.
   b. For example, the action word *list* implies that students can recall a set of terms, whereas the action word *critique* implies that students can evaluate the quality of information presented.
3. A *learning statement* that specifies the learning that will be demonstrated
   a. This statement indicates what the student should know, be able to do, or value.
   b. For example, a chemistry program might have learning statements for knowing the periodic table of elements, being able to communicate scientific findings, and valuing diverse perspectives.

It is important to note that student learning outcomes do not have to be limited to knowledge or skills that can be objectively measured, such as with an exam. You should write outcomes for all of those things that your mission and student learning goals indicate students will learn. For example, if your mission suggests the importance of personal growth and development for your students, then it would be important to reflect this in a student learning goal and at least one associated student learning outcome. When writing outcomes for difficult-to-measure learning, it is especially important that you be intentional in selecting an action word that indicates how you will capture achievement of the learning expressed by the outcome. For example, one effective approach to capturing learning like this is to engage students in a reflection exercise and then apply a rubric to the student responses.

The following examples of student learning outcomes come from a variety of academic programs. It is important to note that each outcome describes who will do the learning (i.e., the opening phrase), tells you what students will do to show you they have learned (i.e., the action word), and expresses exactly what will be learned (i.e., the learning statement).

- Graduates of the program will be able to describe the major subfields of sociology.
- African American studies students will analyze the historical context of primary sources.
- Economics majors will utilize appropriate statistics to test hypotheses.
- Graduates of the program will articulate the personal growth they have experienced through completing their studies.
- Students will reflect on their commitment to making a positive difference in the world.

What Is *Not* a Student Learning Outcome?

Just as it is important to understand the elements that belong in a well-written student learning outcome, it is also important to be able to recognize the elements that should not be included in a learning outcome. Each of the following items are important considerations in designing a program and planning your pedagogy, but they are not learning outcomes because they do not specify what students will know, be able to do, or value by the time they complete the program.

A student learning outcome does *not* include the following:

- What you will offer the student
  - The things you offer your students (e.g., a well-developed library collection) are important to learning but are not equivalent to learning.
- The process a student will go through to learn

o The curriculum and pedagogy that students experience contribute to learning but are not the same as the learning that results from these experiences.
- Student satisfaction with the program
  o Satisfaction is generally important, but just because a student is satisfied does not mean he or she learned anything. Alternatively, it is possible for a student to learn a lot but not be satisfied with the experience.

The following are a few examples of statements that are *not* student learning outcomes:

- Students will be given the opportunity to work as a team.
- The program prepares students for graduate study.
- Students will participate in an internship.
- Graduates will be satisfied with their course work.

If you find yourself with non–outcome statements like these, the simplest way to fix them is to think about what students will get from the experiences you describe and focus your revised learning outcomes on that learning. For example, you could replace the statement that students will have the opportunity to do teamwork with "Students will work effectively in team settings."

Writing Your Student Learning Outcomes

The simplest approach to writing a learning outcome is to generate the learning statement, then determine the action word, and finally add the opening phrase to complete the outcome. The following sections provide approaches to generating a list of essential learning statements for your program and illustrate how you might use learning taxonomies, such as Revised Bloom's Taxonomy (Anderson & Krathwohl, 2001), to determine your action words.

Writing the Learning Statement for a Learning Outcome: Sources of Ideas

Generating a list of learning statements for your program's learning outcomes begins with an examination of your mission statement and student learning goals. Here we review this process and provide a few additional sources of ideas for developing learning statements for your program's learning outcomes.

- Examine your mission statement and student learning goals.
  - o Your mission statement explains why your program exists and offers a holistic vision of the values and philosophy of the program. Program student learning goals are drawn from the mission statement. Student learning goals are broad statements that describe the knowledge, skills, attitudes, and beliefs that graduates of your program should possess. For more on mission statements and learning goals, see module 2.
  - o Use the content of your goals to determine what specific learning you expect students to achieve. For example, if one of your student learning goals says that graduates of the program will be able to conduct independent research, then you would likely write learning statements for information literacy, research methodology, research ethics, and possibly more.
- Check out what professional organizations in your discipline suggest.
  - o Many disciplinary and professional organizations have created statements that define what graduates in the field should be able to do.
    - □ Not every organization refers to these as *learning outcomes*; for example, they may use terms like *learning goals* or *learning objectives*. Just remember that you are looking for statements that describe what a student should know, be able to do, or value upon completion of the program.
  - o If your disciplinary or professional organization has written such statements, then you should tailor the suggested statements about learning to reflect your own curriculum, student learning goals, and mission statement.
- Engage faculty and students in your program in generating ideas for learning statements.
  - o Asking the faculty and the students in your program to engage in conversations about what the curriculum prepares students to know, do, and value can help you to create a list of learning statements.
  - o Engaging faculty and students in the process of developing student learning outcomes can have the benefit of helping to create ownership of and interest in the assessment process that will follow.

Choosing an Action Word for Your Learning Outcomes

Once you've generated a learning statement for an outcome, you'll need to choose an action word to describe how students will demonstrate their accomplishment of the learning. One thing to keep in mind when choosing an action word is that it needs to reflect observable behavior and should even point you toward the type of evidence you need to collect in order to assess student accomplishment of the outcome. As such, you'll want to avoid nonobservable words like *understand* or *know*. If the word *understand* best describes the type of learning that you expect students to accomplish for a particular learning statement, then you'll want to choose an action word that reflects how students will show you that understanding, such as *explain*.

While there are a variety of approaches to choosing an action word, we find it to be most helpful to start by considering the level or type of learning that you expect students to achieve. One way to do this is to examine the levels of learning described by learning taxonomies. Learning taxonomies exist for each of the three domains of learning: kinesthetic, affective, and cognitive. The *kinesthetic*, or *psychomotor*, domain describes learning of physical functions, such as those required to perform a dance movement or assemble circuit boards (e.g., Harrow, 1972). The *affective* domain describes learning in the emotional realm, including things like values, motivations, and attitudes (e.g., Krathwohl, Bloom, & Masia, 1973). The *cognitive* domain focuses on acquisition of knowledge (e.g., Anderson & Krathwohl, 2001). Let's examine how we might use a cognitive taxonomy to determine action words.

Using Revised Bloom's Taxonomy to Choose an Action Word

Revised Bloom's Taxonomy (Anderson & Krathwohl, 2001) can be very helpful with the process of choosing action words because it provides a list of the major types of cognitive learning. Table 3.1 lists the types of learning described by the taxonomy, provides a definition for each type, and provides examples of action words that correspond to each type of learning. To use Revised Bloom's Taxonomy to choose an action word you would determine the type of learning you expect students to achieve by the time they complete your program and then select an appropriate action. For example, if I expect students to be able to understand the relationships among various major theories, I might choose an action word like *compare* or *analyze*.

Putting It Together

After you've written your learning statement and selected your action word, it's time to choose your opening phrase and assemble your student learning outcome. Generally, the same opening phrase is used for each of the program's outcome statements. This will help make it clear that each of the statements belongs to the set and can simplify the process of writing them

TABLE 3.1

Examples of Action Words That Reflect the Types of Learning Described by Revised Bloom's Taxonomy

Type of Learning	Definition	Example Action Words
Remembering	Recalling information	Recognize, name, retrieve, describe, list, define, identify, outline, reproduce
Understanding	Explaining ideas or concepts	Explain, summarize, paraphrase, classify, interpret, distinguish, defend, discuss
Applying	Using information in another situation	Use, execute, carry out, implement, classify, solve, demonstrate, compute
Analyzing	Breaking information into parts to explore understandings and relationships	Analyze, organize, compare, deconstruct, dissect, differentiate, diagram, combine
Evaluating	Justifying a decision or course of action	Judge, critique, experiment, hypothesize, appraise, assess, justify
Creating	Generating new ideas, products, or ways of viewing things	Produce, design, construct, plan, invent, generate, transform, integrate

Note. Adapted from Anderson and Krathwohl (2001).

out. For example, if each of my program's outcomes begins in the same way, then I can present my outcomes like so:

Accounting majors will

- *prepare financial statements in accordance with industry standards,*
- *select courses of action in accordance with ethical standards of the profession, and*
- *deliver a professional accounting presentation.*

A Few Simple Rules for Writing Your Learning Outcomes

Ultimately you will want to have a set of student learning outcomes for your program that are meaningful to both faculty and students. In addition, you'll want your outcomes to be measurable so that you can understand and improve student achievement of them. As such, here are a few rules to help you write meaningful and measurable outcomes. Well-written student learning outcomes will do the following:

- Be jargon free and use clear language.
  - o Your outcomes will be read by a number of audiences, including current students, prospective students, parents, and potential employers of your graduates. Write your outcomes in language that will allow your audience to understand what students in your program learn.
  - o If you find that you must include a specific disciplinary term (i.e., jargon), then include a definition for that term. The definition might be provided parenthetically or in a second sentence.
- Contain only one learning statement.
  - o Understanding achievement of an outcome will be more effective and manageable if each student learning outcome focuses on one element of learning.
- Contain only one action word.
  - o Specify the action associated with the highest or most complex level of learning you expect students to demonstrate. In almost all cases this word will encompass the other action word(s).
  - o For example, in this outcome, "Students will define and apply key terminology," the action word *define* should be removed. The ability to apply terminology correctly includes an understanding of the definition, so there is no need to specify both levels of learning in the outcome.
- Be appropriate, realistic, and attainable.
  - o Students should realistically be able to achieve the learning outcome by completing your program.
  - o In addition, the type of learning expressed in the outcome should be appropriate to the student's level (i.e., undergraduate minor, undergraduate major, graduate student).

Helpful Hints for Writing Your Student Learning Outcomes

We conclude this module on writing your learning outcomes with some helpful hints for writing your program's student learning outcomes.

- Because it is helpful to have multiple perspectives during the process of writing outcomes, we recommend that you work with a small group of two or three faculty members to draft your program's outcomes. Each faculty member may have unique ideas about what the outcomes for students should be. Working in a group allows for conversations and consensus about what students should achieve.

- Once you've drafted a set of learning outcomes, ask the remaining faculty in your program to review the content. Faculty can provide feedback on whether they feel the curriculum prepares students to achieve the list of outcomes you've generated and if they feel any essential learning is missing from the list.

- Before you finalize your learning outcomes, be sure to check that you have phrased your outcomes clearly. A great way to do this is to ask your students as well as faculty from other disciplines if they understand what is intended.

- It is important to note that there is generally not a correct number of student learning outcomes for a program. Some programs have as few as five student learning outcomes; others have a much greater number. There is sometimes a tendency when first developing learning outcomes to write a lot of them, which then creates difficulty in developing a meaningful or manageable assessment plan. The key is to develop a set of outcomes that reflects the knowledge, skills, and values your mission and learning goals indicate are essential. Students should have multiple experiences through completing the curriculum that help them to achieve each learning outcome, which you'll see illustrated in your curriculum map (see module 4, "Curriculum and Outcome Mapping: Understanding the Path to Student Learning in Your Program"). Keeping in mind that your program learning outcomes should reflect essential learning and themes of the curriculum should help you to develop an appropriate and manageable number of outcomes.

- We encourage you to check for any rules you might need to follow regarding learning outcomes. We have encountered institutions that have rules about the required number of learning outcomes for each program. For example, we've met faculty at one institution where every program was required to have exactly six outcomes. Some disciplinary accreditors have requirements about the content or language of learning outcomes. For example, the American Bar Association's *2016–2017 Standards and Rules of Procedure for Approval of Law Schools* specify that accredited schools shall have learning outcomes that at a minimum address a specified set of four broad competencies.

Summary

Articulating student learning outcomes for your program is an essential first step in conducting meaningful assessment. A well-written learning outcome will tell you not only what students are expected to learn but also how they should demonstrate that learning. This helps you to make clear decisions about how to measure that learning and will ultimately help you to determine what types of changes for improvement are necessary.

4

CURRICULUM AND OUTCOME MAPPING

Understanding the Path to Student Learning in Your Program

To improve student learning, you must first understand student learning. That understanding must be as much about *how* your students learn as it is about *what* they learn. Thus, it is important to know where, how often, and how students are encountering the knowledge, skills, and values you want them to learn. This is where a map becomes an invaluable tool. Just like a road map shows you the path that you will travel from home to your destination, maps used in assessment show you the path a student follows through your curriculum from his or her first year to graduation. In this module we describe how to construct the two different types of maps used in assessment: curriculum maps and outcome maps. We'll then share some of the myriad possible uses for your maps.

Curriculum Mapping

A curriculum map is a method for depicting the alignment between a program's curriculum and the student learning outcomes of the program. It is a visual representation of where in your program you foster the desired knowledge, skills, and values.

To begin a curriculum map, create a table in which the learning outcomes for your program are listed down the left-hand column and the required courses are listed across the top row. When complete, you will have a grid in which the learning outcomes comprise the rows and courses comprise the columns, as illustrated in Table 4.1 and Table 4.2.

Once the table has been created, there are two different approaches to filling in the map. These approaches result in either an overview map or a levels map. While you can construct both for your program, you will generally only need one or the other. Each is described next.

TABLE 4.1
Example Overview Map For a Psychology Program

Learning Outcomes	Required Courses									
	Psy 101	Psy 102	Psy 201	Psy 220	Psy 310	Psy 320	Psy 330	Psy 340	Psy 435	Psy 490
Summarize central aspects in the history of psychology.	X			X	X	X	X	X		
Identify biological bases of behavior and development.	X			X	X			X	X	
Outline the major ideas behind the individual differences perspective.	X			X				X	X	
Explain key social factors that influence cognition and behavior.	X			X		X				
Select methodology appropriate to a particular research question generated by the student.			X							X
Distinguish among major statistical tests and be able to choose appropriate tests for specific data sets.		X	X							X
Design research that follows the ethical principles of psychology as established by the APA.	X			X		X		X		X
Write a research report in APA style.			X						X	X
Evaluate scientific research, including research presented in the media.	X	X	X	X	X	X	X		X	X

TABLE 4.2
Example Levels Map For a Psychology Program

Learning Outcomes I = Introduced; D = Developed; M = Mastered	Required Courses									
	Psy 101	Psy 102	Psy 201	Psy 220	Psy 310	Psy 320	Psy 330	Psy 340	Psy 435	Psy 490
Summarize central aspects in the history of psychology.	I			D	D	D	D	D	D	
Identify biological bases of behavior and development.	I			D	D			D	M	
Outline the major ideas behind the individual differences perspective.	I			D			M	M		
Explain key social factors that influence cognition and behavior.	I			D		M				
Select methodology appropriate to a particular research question generated by the student.			I							M
Distinguish among major statistical tests and be able to choose appropriate tests for specific data sets.		I	D							M
Design research that follows the ethical principles of psychology as established by the APA.	I		I			D		D		M
Write a research report in APA style.			I						M	M
Evaluate scientific research, including research presented in the media.	I	I	D	D	D	D	D		M	M

Overview Map

An overview map is an at-a-glance depiction of which outcomes are addressed in each of the required courses. It gives you a sense of how often your students are exposed to content and experiences related to each of your program's learning outcomes as students move through your curriculum. As they are normally the simplest type of map to create, overview maps are a good place to start if it is your first time creating a curriculum map.

To create an overview map, start with the first learning outcome and, proceeding across the row, place a check mark or "X" in each cell where that outcome is addressed in a course. For example, if the learning outcome is "Apply quantitative methods to solve real-world problems" you would likely put a check mark in the cell for a required quantitative statistics course. You then repeat the process for each learning outcome. Table 4.1 shows an example of a completed overview map for a psychology program.

The Temptation of the X

We should note that there is sometimes a temptation on the part of faculty to be liberal with their use of check marks. That is, if a concept, skill, or value is briefly touched on in a course, some faculty want to indicate that the outcome is addressed in that course, perhaps motivated by a desire to show that most or all of the courses in their program address most or all of the learning outcomes. We understand this inclination; however, for your map to be useful, check marks in a curriculum map should reflect an intentional focus on a learning outcome in a given course. Some rules of thumb for determining what qualifies as an intentional focus include the presence of related course-level learning outcomes; a particular module in the course that addresses the outcome; or that student performance on outcome-related assignments, in-class discussions, or activities will contribute in a substantial way to the course grade.

Levels Map

A levels map provides information about the level at which an outcome is addressed in a given course. A levels map gives you a sense of how students' learning grows and deepens as they move through your curriculum. The difference between a levels map and an overview map is in how the cells are populated. Instead of using check marks, you indicate with a letter whether a learning outcome is being introduced (I), developed (D), or mastered (M) in a given course. You might also see reinforced (R) instead of developed and emphasized (E) instead of mastered. Really, any set of designations is fine; it's just a matter of what your faculty feel works best for describing your curriculum.

To give you a sense of how a levels map differs from an overview map, Table 4.2 shows that same psychology curriculum from the outcome map in Table 4.1 now presented in a levels map.

Although the knowledge, skills, and values expressed by a program's learning outcomes are generally introduced in lower division introductory courses, developed through the middle of the curriculum, and mastered in upper division courses, this is not always the case. For example, Psychology Research Methods (Psy 201), an introductory course, might have a "D" associated with the learning outcome "Distinguish among major statistical tests and be able to choose appropriate tests for specific data sets" because this outcome was already introduced in the lower division statistics course preceding it (Psy 102). Similarly, a junior-level course may introduce a concept or skill that students have not encountered in previous courses. The key to constructing a meaningful levels map is to discuss as a faculty what constitutes introducing, developing, or mastering a concept. Keep in mind that in this context *mastery* means a level of learning that is expected of graduates of the program, which is not typically that of a professional in the field. It is our experience that defining the levels in your map can typically be resolved through discussion in a faculty meeting. Once decided, it will help everyone if the definitions are written down and included with the map, as well as shared with all program faculty.

Outcome Mapping

An outcome map focuses on a single student learning outcome. The map is of the significant pedagogies, course content, assignments, and activities for that outcome. It provides rich and detailed information about the range, frequency, and nature of the learning experiences students have related to a learning outcome as they progress through the program. While you will only need one version of a curriculum map for your program, you may make as many outcome maps as you have outcomes. Many programs make a curriculum map to maintain a sense of how students experience the entire curriculum and then choose to make outcome maps for each outcome as they approach its assessment. Outcome mapping at the beginning of an assessment cycle can be very helpful as it is used in multiple steps of the assessment process, including deciding where and what specific evidence of student learning to collect and where and what types of changes for improvement to implement.

The easiest way to create an outcome map is to construct a table for the outcome that lists required courses in one column and significant experiences related to the outcome in the other. Taking one of our example psychology program's outcomes, we constructed the outcome map shown in Table 4.3.

As shown in this example outcome map, significant experiences can include such things as a textbook chapter devoted to the topic; lectures or in-class discussions related to the topic; a substantial assignment, such as a research paper, focused on the content area or skill.

TABLE 4.3.

Example Outcome Map For a Psychology Program's Student Learning Outcomes

Learning Outcome: Design research that follows the ethical principles of psychology as established by the APA.	
Required Courses for Major	**Significant Experiences**
Psy 101: Introduction to Psychology	• Significant portion of one textbook chapter • One lecture and discussion period • One reflection paper
Psy 102: Introduction to Statistics for Psychology	
Psy 201: Psychology Research Methods	• One textbook chapter • One lecture and discussion period • One homework assignment involving case studies
Psy 220: Developmental Psychology	
Psy 310: Cognitive Psychology	
Psy 320: Social Psychology	• One lecture • Research and reflection paper on impact of ethical guidelines on social psychological research
Psy 330: Personality Psychology	
Psy 340: Abnormal Psychology	• One lecture • One film and discussion
Psy 435: Neuropsychology	
Psy 490: Senior Thesis	• In-class discussion • Proposal to the Institutional Review Board (or Human Subjects Review Committee)

Deciding What's Significant

One issue that might arise when creating an outcome map is disagreement among program faculty about how to fill in the cells in the table. There are several possible sources of disagreement. Sometimes it is simply a matter of faculty having different thresholds for what constitutes a significant, or intentional, focus. As noted earlier, some faculty tend to be generous in their use of check marks in an overview map, and as with that case, a negotiation among faculty can usually yield agreement fairly quickly about what should be included in your outcome map.

There is potential for a greater challenge to arise when there are multiple sections of a required course offered by different faculty members. For example, the different instructors might require different textbooks or give very different types of assignments. In this case, it may be more difficult to arrive at agreements about the level with which and by what method the outcome is addressed. One possible resolution is to look at the most common ways in which a learning outcome is addressed across the sections and use that as a guide. Another possible resolution, which could have positive consequences for students' learning experiences, is to come to some agreement about greater consistency across multiple sections in the future.

Filling in Your Map

There are at least three different approaches to populating your map with those check marks, levels indicators, or significant learning experiences. One of these approaches is to do it yourself. You, or perhaps you and a small committee, can collect all of the syllabi for the courses in your curriculum and decide on the type of map you want to create and the rules you will follow to determine what experiences earn an appropriate notation on the map. You then fill in the map. This approach works best if the syllabi in your program tend to contain a great deal of detail, especially including course learning outcomes; assignment descriptions; and a schedule of course readings, topics, and activities.

Another possible approach is to give each faculty member the map with instructions for filling it in for the courses that they teach. Faculty then send back their completed map to the designated point person, who compiles all responses into a complete map. Provided instructions are clear, and faculty follow them (e.g., avoiding the temptation to say that they address all outcomes in all their courses), this approach can be a big time-saver. The downside of this approach is that faculty will tend not to engage with each other in meaningful discussion of what is happening across the curriculum.

A final approach—and to be honest, our favorite approach—is for the program faculty to work as a whole to fill in the map. We like this approach because it engages the entire faculty in meaningful conversation about the curriculum. Everyone brings his or her syllabi and talks about what he or she does to teach students the knowledge, skills, and values expressed by the program's learning outcomes. We have helped to run many such meetings and as a result have learned that too often each faculty member teaches his or her own courses without a clear understanding of what's going on in the other courses in the curriculum. The conversations that happen as the map gets filled in often result in faculty deciding on necessary changes to their courses in order to improve student learning—all before any formal assessment of that learning has taken place. For example, a faculty member might learn that a topic she assumed she was reinforcing is not actually introduced in the curriculum prior to her course and realize that a different approach is needed. Or a faculty member realizes he doesn't need to spend time introducing a topic because it's covered in a prior course, thus freeing up time to focus on other key topics. It is important to note that because this approach to filling in your map tends to engage faculty in rich discussions of teaching and learning it can require a longer meeting to get it done. If this is the approach you take, we recommend allowing at least a couple of hours for the task, which might mean that you need to break the work up over a few meetings during an academic year, or plan to get it done during a longer retreat.

No matter which approach you use to fill in your map, once complete, we recommend that you take the final, filled-in map to the full program faculty for consideration. A review by the entire faculty will help you to make sure that you've captured things correctly.

Uses for Curriculum and Outcome Maps

Beyond providing an understanding of how your program's curriculum addresses your student learning outcomes, curriculum and outcome maps can be used in several ways during the assessment process and beyond. While we list a few of the most popular uses next, we know there are many more possibilities. This is because, while relatively simple, maps provide rich information about your curriculum and pedagogy that can help you with a number of program activities, including things like helping you explain to adjunct faculty the role the course they will teach plays in the overall curriculum, and successfully completing academic program review.

Conduct a Preliminary Assessment

One of the advantages of curriculum maps is that they allow you to see at a glance whether there are any gaps in your curriculum. That is, by looking for patterns in the blank spaces in a curriculum map you can determine if one (or more) of your learning outcomes is not covered in the curriculum. An extreme example would be if the row for one of your learning outcomes has no check marks in it. Although rare, this does happen, typically with less clearly defined learning outcomes such as critical thinking. A less extreme example might be if the row for a learning outcome contains one "I" and one "D" but no "M." Both cases suggest that the learning outcome is not fully addressed (or addressed at all). As a result, you might consider making changes to your curriculum or pedagogy, even before collecting any assessment data.

Alternatively, you might find a blank column in your curriculum map. This could suggest that the course needs revision so that it addresses existing learning outcomes, or it might suggest that your outcomes are not consistent with what is happening in your curriculum. That is, perhaps there is some knowledge or skill that faculty want students to learn (and is addressed in that course with a blank column) but it has not been made explicit as a program student learning outcome. As a result, you might consider refining the list of learning outcomes for your program to describe more accurately the desired learning in the program.

In some programs the exercise of mapping reveals that it's possible for students to avoid exposure to certain learning outcomes. This happens most often when students are allowed to select a certain number of classes from a menu to fulfill unit requirements for the major, such as requiring students to take any 3 upper division courses from a set of 10 possible courses. In this case, grouping those courses by the learning outcomes they address in common and requiring students to take a course from each of those groupings can help to ensure that students have an opportunity to achieve each of the program's student learning outcomes.

Determine When, Where, and How to Gather Evidence

Curriculum maps provide information about where an outcome is addressed in your curriculum. In addition, outcome maps tell you the methods with which it is addressed. As a result, curriculum maps and outcome maps can be very helpful in determining what evidence of student learning in which courses to gather. For example, looking at the levels map in Table 4.2, we can see that the senior-most course where students demonstrate mastery of the major ideas behind the individual differences perspective occurs in the junior year (Psy 340). That tells us that we will want to look to that course to see if there is an appropriate writing assignment that we could collect and apply a rubric to, or perhaps there is an exam that we could include items for program assessment in.

Determine Where to Make Changes for Improvement

Outcome maps are particularly useful for identifying opportunities for improvement after you have determined what your assessment evidence tells you about student learning. For example, you might have administered a senior exit exam and results show that students performed at a less than desired level on interpreting tables and graphs. By reviewing a map of that outcome you might see that although interpretation of tables and graphs was covered in a book chapter and two lecture and discussion periods in the introductory statistics course there were no significant experiences related to this outcome in the research methods course or required upper division courses. This observation suggests there are opportunities for adding or enhancing learning experiences related to this outcome in one or more courses. Additional examples of using maps to identify where and how to make changes for improvement are described in module 11, "Closing the Loop: Interpreting Results and Taking Action."

Summary

Curriculum and outcome maps are incredibly versatile and helpful tools. The process of making a map can reveal important information about teaching and learning across your curriculum and can even lead you to make informed changes for improvement before you've formally looked at evidence of student learning. Once created, maps have a number of possible uses, including where to find relevant student work for assessment of each outcome, and where to implement changes for improvement at the end of each assessment cycle.

5

PLANNING

Creating a Meaningful and Manageable Assessment Plan for Your Program

Let's face it. Assessment involves work. If it is done well, it is work that easily fits within your already numerous responsibilities, all the while helping you to improve teaching and learning in your program. That is to say, the work of assessment should be both manageable and meaningful. In order for the work of assessment to be done in a meaningful, manageable, and sustainable way, you need a plan. Assessment plans do not have to be complex documents. Essentially, an assessment plan notes who does what when. In this module, we'll look at reasons for planning, the essential elements of a plan, how to document your plan, and share a few tips for making the planning process work for you and your colleagues.

Why Plan?

One of the reasons people resist assessment is that they perceive it as an all-or-nothing activity. They seem to think that they have to do everything all the time. In other words, they feel like they must focus on every outcome and complete every step in the assessment process every academic term. This all-or-nothing approach would not make for very effective assessment; after all, it would not be very manageable, nor would it allow time for your program faculty to engage with each student learning outcome in a meaningful way. One very good reason to plan is that you set yourself up for a manageable approach to assessment. You pick one or two outcomes to start work on each year and lay out the necessary steps over one to two academic years. Once you have completed the first round of assessment of all of your program's student learning outcomes, you will cycle back and reassess your outcomes. Knowing that all of your outcomes will be assessed on a cycle and seeing that work broken into manageable steps to be completed each academic term can alleviate that sense of having to do it all right now.

In addition to distributing the work of assessment over time in your plan, you can distribute responsibility for each step. Assigning different faculty members to each task makes sure that no one is overwhelmed with too many things to do. In addition, as people are involved in the project, you will see an increase in investment in the process. After all, anytime you help with a project, you tend to be more interested in its results. While assigning responsibilities, be sure to assign a lead faculty member for each student learning outcome. The lead faculty member will be tasked with reminding others of steps that need to be taken each term, answering questions about the process, and making sure the process stays on track.

One final great reason to plan is that it serves as a record of what has been done. As we saw in the assessment cycle described in module 1, you will eventually circle back and assess each outcome again. Having a clear record of the plan that you followed will be very helpful in carrying out that next cycle. You will know exactly what happened and can decide if you want to replicate it or modify it. For more great reasons to keep a record, check out module 12, "Record Keeping: Keeping Track of Your Work," which goes into detail about all of the things you should keep records of and why it is important to keep records of the entire assessment process.

A Note for Small Programs

If you are in a small program you may not have many other colleagues to share the responsibilities of completing the assessment process. Despite the fact that there are not many of you to spread the responsibilities around, there are still ways to keep the process manageable. One approach that works well is to collaborate with the faculty in another small program. This partnership approach gives you a few options. For example, you could design a joint plan working on similar outcomes. While the exact phrasing of your outcomes might differ, the core ideas within them might be highly related, allowing you to design a process that works for both of you. We have seen this work for outcomes related to writing, speaking, critical thinking, interdisciplinary knowledge, and more. In this approach, you lay out your plan so that you work together on as many steps as possible, including steps like designing a rubric, applying the rubric to student work, and discussing what the results are telling you.

Another approach that we have seen work well for small programs working together is to trade off years. For example, in odd years you work together to complete the assessment steps for a student learning outcome of your program, and in even years you work to complete the steps for the other program. In this case, one program takes the lead, while the other provides assistance with steps like designing a rubric, applying that rubric to student work, and making sense of the findings.

If the partnership approach will not work for you, consider instead forming a committee of faculty from other programs at your institution. It is ideal to invite colleagues who teach courses that are affiliated with your program, such as through cross-listing, to join. That said, even colleagues who are not affiliated with your program but are available to invest their time and expertise to assist you will be valuable committee members. The role your committee plays is up to you and your colleagues to define. We have seen the committee approach be highly effective when the committee serves essentially as an advisory board, helping you think through assessment plans, reviewing drafts of assessment measurement tools like rubrics, and thinking through your findings with you. We have also seen this work when committee members are involved in carrying out just about every step in the plan. Whatever your needs may be, your assessment plan will be more likely to stay on track and your committee members will be most effective if you have established a clearly defined set of responsibilities for your committee.

What Goes Into a Plan?

As with many assessment activities, there are no concrete rules about exactly what goes into a plan. That said, to assess each of your student learning outcomes there are certain steps that need to be completed. An effective assessment plan lays out when each of these steps will be undertaken and who will be involved in carrying them out.

When generating a plan, it is important to decide which student learning outcome, or outcomes, you will focus on each year. To keep the work of assessment manageable we recommend that you plan to undertake the assessment of one or, at most, two outcomes each year. If you are new to assessment, we believe it is good practice to start by focusing on only one student learning outcome in the first year. This will give you a chance to learn the assessment process and what works for your program.

There are six steps involved in completing the assessment of each of your student learning outcomes:

1. Selecting the evidence
2. Collecting the evidence
3. Scoring the evidence
4. Analyzing the scores
5. Interpreting the findings

6. Taking action as needed

We have illustrated what these might look like in an assessment plan in Table 5.1. Let's take a deeper look at exactly what each step entails.

Selecting the Evidence

This step involves determining what you will collect from students that demonstrates achievement of the student learning outcome (i.e., your evidence) and then developing the assessment measurement tool that will allow you to measure the evidence to determine how well students are accomplishing the outcome. The evidence you select should make sense given both the action word and the learning statement expressed by your student learning outcome. For example, if you want to understand achievement of your written communication outcome, then it makes the most sense to plan to collect student papers submitted as part of a course. If you want to understand achievement of a factual knowledge outcome, then it typically makes sense to collect exams from a course where students are asked to master that knowledge.

To determine where the evidence might exist, look to your curriculum or outcome map (as described in module 4, "Curriculum and Outcome Mapping: Understanding the Path to Student Learning in Your Program"). Generally, you will want to look to the senior-most course in your curriculum that addresses the outcome. The reasons for this are to ensure that students have had ample opportunity to achieve the outcome before you assess and that students have achieved it prior to graduation.

Collecting evidence that already exists is referred to as embedded assessment. There are many benefits to embedded assessment. One important benefit is that students will most likely be demonstrating their best performance as they have submitted the work for a grade within a course. Students tend to take graded assignments more seriously and put more of an effort forward than they would in a situation where they are asked to generate a paper, or other type of assignment, or take an exam for a nongraded program assessment activity. Another benefit of utilizing embedded assessments is that they reduce the amount of work that faculty need to do to assess outcomes. In other words, instead of having to generate the assignment or exam, that assignment or exam already exists and at most will need modification.

Once you have determined what evidence you will collect, you need to develop the assessment measurement tool that you will use to extract information about the outcome from that evidence. There are two basic types of assessment measurement tools for extracting information from embedded assessment: exams and rubrics. Obviously, if you have selected an exam, then you need exam items and a key for scoring these. In this case, review the

TABLE 5.1.

Example Assessment Plan Documented in a Table

Outcome	Activity	Fall 2018	Spring 2019	Fall 2019	Spring 2020
Students will effectively communicate their ideas in writing utilizing disciplinary style conventions.	Selecting the evidence	*Dana & Pat create rubric to apply to research papers from 450 course*			
	Collecting the evidence	*Pat collects electronic papers from 450 course*			
	Scoring the evidence		*Dana & Frances (early in semester)*		
	Analyzing the scores		*Dana (by midsemester)*		
Lead: Dana	Interpreting the findings		*ALL FACULTY (final meeting)*		
	Taking action			*As needed . . .*	
Students will solve problems through the application of fundamental theoretical principles.	Selecting the evidence		*Taylor & Sam generate exam items & scoring key for 420 course*		
	Collecting the evidence		*Sam will scan student exam responses prior to grading*		
	Scoring the evidence			*Sam & Charlie (over summer or early fall)*	
	Analyzing the scores			*Dana (by midsemester)*	
Lead: Taylor	Interpreting the findings			*ALL FACULTY (final meeting)*	
	Taking action				*As needed . . .*

Note. This plan presents steps taken over four academic terms for two outcomes.

existing exam, determine which items on it speak to your student learning outcome, and decide if additional items are needed to fully capture achievement of that outcome. You can find instructions for developing exam items in module 8, "Exams: Asking Questions That Provide the Answers You Need." If you have selected some other form of student work, such as a paper, a presentation, an art piece, or another type of product that students create, then you will need to develop a rubric. Instructions for developing and using rubrics are shared in module 7, "Rubrics: Creating and Using Rubrics for Program Assessment."

A third type of assessment measurement tool, surveys, is considered an indirect measure of learning and can be used to help understand student achievement of just about every student learning outcome. Surveys are primarily intended as a supplement to a direct measure of learning, such as that generated by a rubric or an exam. Direct and indirect measurement are discussed in the next module, and instructions for designing surveys for assessment can be found in module 9, "Surveys: Finding Out What Your Students Think."

Collecting the Evidence

This is often the easiest step in the entire assessment cycle. After all, you've already selected the evidence, now you just need to go get it. Ideally, your plan will note what course the assignment exists in, the date it will be available, and who will collect it. If possible, assign the faculty member who is teaching the course the work will come from to collect the student work. It is also important to consider whether the work will be graded prior to collection and the format of what you are collecting.

Graded or Ungraded Work

As a general rule, you want to plan to collect unmarked student work. This is so that when you apply the rubric or exam key to the work, you are not biased by comments or scores provided by the faculty member who graded the assignment. Seeing the grade and the notes that the faculty member wrote on the paper may influence how you view the work, reducing your ability to be unbiased.

For the assessment process, there is no benefit to knowing how each student was graded on the assignment. After all, faculty grade students on a number of factors related to achievement within the course. In contrast, the assessment process you are undertaking focuses on understanding student learning outcome achievement. While the course content and the program's student learning outcome will have things in common, the assessment process has different foci than the grading process and should be kept separate. For example, you might be collecting an assignment that the faculty member graded based on how well students understood a historical period, while you are looking at the work to determine student ability to incorporate a mixture of primary and secondary source material in constructing an argument.

When it comes to exams, it can make a lot of sense to collect graded exam items from faculty if there are objective correct answers to each of the outcome-relevant items, such as there would be for multiple-choice items. In this case, the faculty member can share copies of the graded exams or provide the exam item scores.

Format

It is important to consider whether you will collect paper or electronic copies of student work, and plan accordingly. When possible, we recommend collecting electronic copies. It is easier to redact student information from electronic copies, which can help to reduce potential bias when you score the work with a rubric. In addition, electronic copies are easier to share among faculty involved in the scoring of that work. You should note that even if the faculty member whose course the work comes from prefers that students submit paper copies for grading that faculty member can also ask students for electronic copies of their work. In cases where the assignment is generated on paper in class, such as with exams, the paper can be scanned to generate an electronic copy.

For some types of student work, the faculty member collecting that work may need to create a photo or video electronic record. This record will allow faculty to apply the rubric at a later time. For example, a video record of student presentations, performances, and demonstrations will need to be made, and student artwork will need to be photographed. This electronic record does not need to be of professional quality. The recording will serve its purpose as long as it is a clear recording. Most of us have smartphones with cameras capable of making such recordings; however, if you do not have a camera available in the program, then check to see if you can borrow one. We have found on many campuses cameras are available to borrow from the library or the information technology (IT) department.

A Note About Live Presentations and Performances

You might be wondering why we are suggesting that you record live presentations and performances to be scored at a later time with your rubric. After all, you could plan to have the faculty member who is teaching the course apply the rubric at the time of the presentation, performance, or demonstration, thus saving everyone some time. While scoring "live" is possible, it is incredibly difficult to do, especially if you are also trying to grade the student on stage, keep an eye on the other students in class, and come up with questions to ask the presenting student when they have finished (i.e., teach the class). In addition, with a live presentation or performance it is very possible to miss things. You lower your eyes to write something down, which diverts your attention for a moment, and before you know it you've missed something that was important for determining the correct rubric score. So, while it is possible to score in the moment, it is not an easy or ideal practice.

Scoring the Evidence

This step involves scoring the exam items, applying the rubric to the collected student work, or scoring survey responses. Specific steps for how to approach these tasks are included in the modules on these topics (modules 7–9). For planning purposes, what is important to note is that except in cases where there is an objective correct answer, such as on a true-false exam item, more than one person will ideally participate in scoring the work. When there is not a clear correct answer, scoring is somewhat subjective. Involving multiple perspectives in the process can help to ensure an agreed-on and consistent scoring process.

Analyzing the Scores

The best part about analyzing the scores is that that there is not one correct way to approach the task. You have to do what makes sense for your program. If you are a faculty that likes tables, generate one. If you like graphs, go for it. If a paragraph summarizing overall patterns observed makes the most sense for you, do it. If you need more guidance on how to approach this step, module 10, "Organizing, Summarizing, and Presenting Your Evidence: Using Microsoft Excel to Make Sense of Your Data," presents step-by-step instructions for using the software to organize, summarize, and present your assessment data.

Interpreting the Findings

This is one step that needs to include the entire program faculty working together. Certainly, the faculty who analyzed the scores may have a sense of what their analysis tells you about student learning, but it is essential that everyone be included in a conversation about what the findings mean and what, if anything, should be done because of those findings. In module 11, "Closing the Loop: Interpreting Results and Taking Action," we share ideas for how to engage in this meaningful discussion of findings.

Taking Action as Needed

This step is the only one that you cannot really assign someone to complete. The actions you take as a result of assessment will depend on what program faculty have decided as a whole. It is still important to note when this step will take place, and you might even note that the person charged with leading assessment of the student learning outcome will verify that changes were made.

Documenting Your Plan

While there are many possible ways to document the plan you have outlined, we find that a simple table is the most effective way to create a clear record. Essentially, your table functions a lot like a calendar with a to-do list, making it easy to follow as you carry out your plan. In addition, the tabular format makes it easy to communicate your plan both to those program faculty not involved in developing the plan and to interested constituencies outside of your program. Those constituencies might include your dean's office, your institution's program review committee, or your disciplinary or regional accrediting body.

In a tabular format, the columns of your assessment plan represent academic terms. Each student learning outcome in your plan represents a row, which is then further broken into the tasks that need to be completed. Within each cell of the table you can note more details about the task to be completed, as well as note who is to be responsible for completing each task. You can create assessment plan tables that cover as many outcomes and as many academic terms as you need, or create a separate table for each outcome or academic year. Tabular assessment plans can be easily created in Microsoft Word or Microsoft Excel. We shared an example of what a tabular plan might look like in Table 5.1.

Example Plan

In Table 5.1, we have laid out a plan covering two academic years (i.e., four semesters), and two student learning outcomes. The example program will begin the assessment of its written communication outcome in the fall term, Fall 2018, and Dana will take the lead on making sure that the program stays on track with the completion of the assessment steps. In that first fall semester, Dana will work with Pat to create the rubric that they will apply to papers from Pat's 450 course. Pat will ask students to submit electronic copies of their papers and share the files with Dana. As the papers are due near the end of the fall semester, the rubric will be applied to them early in the spring 2019 semester. Dana and Frances will complete the rubric scoring task together. Dana, who has the strongest data analysis skills in the program, will then analyze the scores by midsemester so that the findings can be discussed at the final faculty meeting of the semester. Any changes that need to be implemented will go into effect by the following fall.

Our sample assessment plan shows that the program has planned to begin the assessment of a second learning outcome during the second semester, Spring 2019. This second outcome is about solving problems through application of fundamental theoretical principles, something students are asked to master in the 420 course. For this reason, the program faculty have decided that an exam in the 420 course is the best way to capture achievement. Taylor is taking the lead on this outcome. During the spring semester Taylor and Sam, who teaches the 420 course, will work together to construct items for the final exam, an exam key for the closed-ended items, and a rubric for the open-ended items. Sam will scan completed student exams prior to grading them so that they have a clear copy for assessment purposes. Either over the summer or early in the fall, Sam and Charlie will work together to score the exam items and give the scores to Dana for analysis. During the faculty meeting following Dana's analysis (likely the final meeting of the semester), the faculty will discuss the findings and plan any necessary changes. As needed, those changes will be implemented in the following spring semester, Spring 2020.

Tips for Effective Planning

Creating a plan in which your program finds meaning, can manage, and will sustain is essential. Here we share a few tips for achieving a meaningful, manageable, and sustainable assessment plan:

- Plan to focus on only one or two student learning outcomes at a time. This will help you avoid possible "all-or-nothing" feelings, while keeping the workload for each academic term and person involved manageable. In addition, by focusing on only one or two outcomes at a time, you will be able to really focus your attention on those selected outcomes and develop a meaningful understanding of student achievement.
- To get started, pick the student learning outcomes that are most important to you to assess now, and then plan to begin assessment of one or two additional outcomes each year. If you are not certain which outcomes are important, ask your faculty colleagues. Typically, there is at least one outcome that program faculty are concerned that

students may not be fully achieving, one that they are particularly confident students achieve, or one that they are just plain curious about. Interest in the outcome itself can help to increase both interest and involvement in the assessment process.

- o Alternatively, especially if you are new to assessment as a program, you might consider which student learning outcome is easiest to assess and start with that one. For example, if you have a knowledge outcome and an existing exam with items that will work well as evidence, then start there. The experience of completing the assessment process will help increase understanding of the process and ease you into making it a sustainable part of your program's activity.

- If you are planning to assess two student learning outcomes at the same time, try to aim for outcomes that complement each other, and may even be demonstrated by students in the same piece of evidence. For example, if you are collecting papers to understand your critical reasoning learning outcome, then you might also look at the quality of the writing. This would give you evidence for both the critical reasoning and writing outcomes and could reduce the amount of time and effort involved in completing the assessment process.

- Be sure to include sufficient time for each step of your assessment plan. For example, designing a rubric can sometimes take a full semester to complete. Very often, the student work we select as evidence is not submitted until the end of a semester, which does not leave time to apply the rubric during that semester.

- Complete the assessment process in a reasonable amount of time. While you want to allow sufficient time for each step in your plan, you also want to be sure to get it done. Give your program a year to two years to complete all of the assessment steps for each of your student learning outcomes.

- Lay out a timeline for when you will begin the assessment of each of your student learning outcomes and when you will begin to cycle back through your outcomes, but develop the specific plan details for only three to five years into the future. Assessment will help your program to use evidence to continually evolve, which means that after a handful of years your curriculum or your outcomes may look slightly different. It makes sense to develop only the specific details of exactly who will do specifically what for just a few years at a time.

- Keep your program's assessment plan in a shared location, such as in a shared computer drive or cloud file. You want to make sure that everyone can access the assessment plan file to understand what is going on that academic term and check on his or her responsibilities. If the file is stored on one person's computer and that person is not around for a while (say, they are teaching abroad that semester), then no one knows what he or she is supposed to do and the assessment plan may be derailed.

- Include the assessment plan on the agenda for every program faculty meeting. In most meetings, this will require only a quick update by the lead faculty for each outcome that you are actively assessing. In other meetings, you will spend time discussing the findings for an outcome, or working through details of the plan of the next outcome. A major benefit of having the assessment plan on every agenda is that it helps to build a culture in which assessment is a regular part of the business of the program and is everyone's responsibility.

- Keep in mind that the purpose of assessment is to both understand and improve student learning. Staying focused on this goal can help you stay motivated.

Summary

There are a number of great reasons to develop an assessment plan before embarking on an assessment process. Chief among those reasons is that it will help you approach assessment in a manageable way, which can help to increase the meaningfulness of the entire process. An assessment plan indicates who does what when for each of the steps in an assessment process. It is important to keep your plan in a shared place as part of your assessment record. You will find more information about record keeping in module 12, "Record Keeping: Keeping Track of Your Work."

6

ASSESSMENT MEASUREMENT TOOLS

Determining What Your Students Are Learning

R ubrics and exams and surveys, oh my! There is definitely no shortage of possibilities for how to measure student learning. It can sometimes feel as if the number of options is overwhelming. Fortunately, there are good approaches to selecting the most effective assessment measurement tool for understanding accomplishment of your student learning outcomes. In this module we'll go over some of the things you should look for when deciding on an assessment measurement tool, including properties of measurement tools and categories that you should consider, and review the pros and cons of the most commonly used types of assessment measurement tools.

A Few Things to Keep in Mind

When selecting an approach to measuring student accomplishment of a program learning outcome, there are three key things to keep in mind. First, it is essential that the evidence of student learning that you choose to use captures learning that occurs as a result of the program curriculum. This means that evidence of learning should be collected at a point in the curriculum when students have completed all courses that address the relevant knowledge, skills, or values. As a result, most evidence will be collected in the junior or senior year. Your curriculum map can help you to identify these points (see module 4, "Curriculum and Outcome Mapping: Understanding the Path to Student Learning in Your Program"). In addition, when selecting or designing your measurement tool, such as your rubric or exam items, you want to make sure that your assessment measurement tool focuses on content that is actually taught in the program's curriculum. It would not be effective to use a tool that measures general knowledge or information that must be picked up elsewhere.

Second, keep in mind that many assessment measurement tools can be used for multiple levels of assessment. It is how you use the tool that makes the difference. For example, you could use a rubric to grade students, computing a total score to provide a grade and feedback to each student about his or her learning. You could also use a rubric to understand student accomplishment of a program learning outcome by aggregating scores across students on each component of the rubric. Both the approach to looking at the rubric scores as well as the contents of the rubrics would differ. In a rubric used for grading a student paper you'd probably include components for things like grammar and assignment-specific requirements, whereas for program assessment your rubric would focus on only the components of the learning outcome being assessed. For more on how to design and use rubrics for program assessment, check out module 7, "Rubrics: Creating and Using Rubrics for Program Assessment."

Third, some types of evidence of learning are not appropriate for program-level assessment. For example, while grades or overall exam scores are incredibly helpful in understanding some important things about your students and your program, they are not useful for understanding student learning outcome achievement. A grade, much like an overall exam score, combines multiple elements into one score. That single score does not tell you exactly which components of your learning outcome students have mastered and which may need improvement. In other words, that score does not lend itself to action for improvement. For more on how to design and use exams for program assessment, check out module 8, "Exams: Asking Questions That Provide the Answers You Need."

An additional type of evidence that has many great uses but is not appropriate for assessment of program student learning outcomes is the satisfaction survey. Satisfaction surveys can tell you a great deal of important information about your program, but they fail to let you know if students have learned. We've encountered, and are sure you have too, students who were thrilled with their educational experience but didn't seem to learn much. The reverse is also true, in that there are plenty of students who complain about the amount of work required of them or the rigor of the curriculum but have learned a great deal. If you are already using a satisfaction survey, we encourage you to consider modifying it to include questions about your students' perception of their learning and their learning-related behaviors. For more on designing surveys that serve as assessment measurement tools, see module 9, "Surveys: Finding Out What Your Students Think."

Properties of Good Assessment Measurement

In an ideal world, all assessment measurement tools would be perfect. They would measure accurately every time, they would not require much work on the part of faculty or students, and we would always be able to reach a clear set of conclusions leading to actions for improvement. In the real world, no measurement tool is perfect. There is always some degree of error in assessment measurement. But do not despair! You will be able to make or choose very good measurement tools by looking for the properties of good assessment described next. The key is to strive for measurement tools that have as many of these properties as possible, while balancing out which properties are most important to you. For example, perhaps having a time-saving, cost-effective measurement tool is more important to you than having multiple measures that you can triangulate in order to develop a detailed, multifaceted picture of student learning. Recognizing your priorities in this way can help you to select the best tool for the job.

Reliability

While there are multiple types of reliability that can be examined, in general it is the case that a reliable measure gives you the same score each time you use it, unless, of course, there has been some change in what you are measuring. A simple example of a reliable measurement tool is a tape measure. Each time you use that tape measure to determine your height, it should give you the same number—unless you grew or shrank. In fact, that ability to give the same measurement on multiple testings is known as test-retest reliability. In conducting assessment it is relatively rare that we apply the same measurement to a student without expecting there to have been some change. For example, we might apply a rubric (our assessment measurement tool) to papers that students wrote in their first year of college, and then apply that same rubric to papers those students wrote in their last year of college. In this case we'd expect that our measurement tool would reliably capture the growth in learning that has occurred as a result of completing your program's curriculum.

Assuming you are not giving students the same exam repeatedly or scoring multiple papers written during the same semester from each student using the same rubric, the simplest way to look for test-retest reliability is to look for an improvement in scores from the first application of the measure to the next. You should see a pattern across students of general improvement. If you do not see improvement or, even worse, you see a decline in learning, then include in your discussion of results that the issue may be with the measurement tool. While it can be frustrating to find that your measurement tool was not reliable, you can be reassured that this does happen to even the most experienced rubric designers. As described in module 11, "Closing the Loop: Interpreting Results and Taking Action," changing your assessment measurement tool is one of the actions available to you as you make decisions about what the evidence you've examined tells you.

Another type of reliability that can be useful in designing or selecting an assessment measurement tool is parallel forms reliability. Parallel forms reliability is evidenced when we have two or more versions of the assessment measurement tool, and no matter which version is applied the same score is found. This would be like having two different tape measures that both give the same number when you measure your height. We see parallel forms reliability most often being examined as part of an assessment process when a program chooses to make multiple versions of the same exam, perhaps by changing the order of items on the exam or by using slightly different examples in the questions. There are many reasons for designing more than one version of an exam, with the most common being that it is a way to prevent (or reduce) the possibility of cheating during the exam. If the exams have parallel forms reliability, then a student's performance on that exam should not be impacted by the version of the exam that he or she took.

If you are planning to use multiple versions of an assessment tool, you can set yourself up to check for parallel forms reliability by randomly distributing the versions so that you have approximately equal groups with each version. In other words, all of your A students do not receive one version, while all of your C students receive the other. The simplest approach for checking whether you have parallel forms reliability on an exam is to look at performance on each of the parallel items. If an item is consistent across forms you should see similar performance patterns. If it is not consistent you'd see things like every student getting one version of the item correct and only a handful getting the other version correct.

Yet another type of reliability that is regularly looked for when conducting assessment has to do with the people applying the measurement tool. This form of reliability is known as interrater reliability. The basic idea is that the measurement tool and the instructions for how to apply that tool are so clear and well designed that no matter who applies the tool the same score will be found. If we have interrater reliability it will not matter if you or your colleague down the hall measures your height with the tape measure; you'll both get the same number. Interrater reliability is especially important to examine when you have multiple people scoring student work that does not have a single, clear correct answer, such as when you are applying a rubric to student work.

As described in module 7, "Rubrics: Creating and Using Rubrics for Program Assessment," the process of norming can help to increase interrater reliability. A simple way to check for interrater reliability is to have two faculty members independently apply the rubric (or other measurement tool) to the same piece of student work. If you have perfect interrater reliability, the two sets of scores will be the same. If not, more work is likely needed to come to agreement about how to apply the measurement tool.

Validity

Just as with reliability, there is more than one type of validity that can be examined. Regardless of the type of validity, a valid measure is one that measures what it is supposed to. A valid tape measure will tell you your height. A tape measure that lacks validity will tell you something else, like your IQ or your hair color.

The simplest form of validity to examine, face validity, is the idea that the content of your assessment measurement tool looks, on its face, like it measures the knowledge, skill, or value it is supposed to. An American tape measure with face validity, for example, would have markings for inches and feet on it. Face validity is determined by examining the content of your assessment measurement tool, focusing on each and every item or component of that tool. If an item or component does not appear to measure the relevant knowledge, skill, or value, then consider that it may need to be modified or removed in order to improve face validity.

Beyond face validity, a good measure has content validity. When an assessment measure has content validity it means that the content of the measurement tool is both relevant to the outcome being assessed and representative of the knowledge, skills, and values that were taught. In other words, you include only knowledge, skills, and values that are relevant to your outcome and you make sure that all of the essential knowledge, skills, and values that are emphasized throughout your curriculum are included. To examine content validity in your measure, you begin by listing out all of the outcome-related essential knowledge, skills, and values that students should have learned through completing the program. Then you check the items or components of your assessment measurement tool to verify that each thing on your list is represented. Ideally, you will make your list of those essential things students should have learned before you design or select your assessment measurement tool. This way you can make sure that content validity is built in to your assessment measurement tool.

Reliability and Validity and Error

Reliability and validity have an interesting relationship. In order for a measure to be valid, it must be reliable; that is, the measure must produce consistent scores in order for that measurement to be correctly representing what's going on. Yet, a reliable measure is not necessarily valid; that is, just because it produces the same score every time does not mean that score represents what's really happening in the world. For example, if your tape measure consistently tells you that you are 10 feet tall, then you are getting a reliable measure that lacks accuracy.

Yet, even if you have the most reliable and valid measure there is, you will not have a perfect measure. In fact, all measurements of learning contain at least some error, which is to say that they also measure material that is not the learning you are after. There are two primary sources of measurement error. The first, known as systematic error, comes from your measurement tools. For example, if a question on an exam is not perfectly clear, then students may answer the item incorrectly even though they know the information that is being asked for by the question. The second type of measurement error is known as random error and comes from unknown and unpredictable places. For example, a fire alarm going off in the middle of your exam would be a source of random error in student performance on that exam.

While you can't stop a fire alarm from going off, there are steps you can take to reduce the amount of error that gets captured by your measurement tool and process. Systematic error can be reduced by following best practice in designing your assessment measurement tool. One important best practice to reduce systematic error is testing your measurement tool with a small group of students or faculty prior to using it for assessment. This pilot test will help you identify sources of systematic error that you can remove. Random error is virtually impossible to control, but you can still take steps to reduce its possible impact. One way that you can reduce the impact of random error is through using multiple measurements of learning and examining how the results converge to tell you a story about student learning. You might, for example, use both an exam to test learning and a survey to examine learning-related behaviors. Or you might choose to have students put together a portfolio of their work so that you can see multiple examples of how they demonstrate relevant learning.

Actionable

Beyond being reliable and valid, an important property of assessment measurement tools is that they provide actionable evidence. To be actionable means that the results should give you some idea about what to do with them. This property comes from both the design of your measurement tools and the way that you present the findings. It is one of the primary reasons why we recommend that you break your outcome down into its component parts as a first step in developing your assessment measurement tools (see modules 7–9). It is also why we recommend that you organize and present your findings by rubric component, exam item, or survey item (see module 10, "Organizing,

Summarizing, and Presenting Your Evidence: Using Microsoft Excel to Make Sense of Your Data"). These steps provide insight into which components are meeting expectations and which are in need of improvement, thus pointing you toward the actions you need to take for improvement.

Manageable

Ideal assessment measurement tools are efficient and cost effective in terms of both time and money. In other words, good assessment measurement is manageable. This property of good assessment measurement tools comes primarily from decisions you make about the process. For example, before taking a semester and several meetings to develop a rubric from scratch, ask around to see if one already exists that you could modify for program assessment. It is very possible that a colleague in your program or in a program like yours at another institution has exactly what you are looking for. Or if you are considering using an exam, before you decide to pay for students to take an expensive standardized exam (or ask students to pay for it), consider working together as a faculty to develop your own exam.

Interesting and Meaningful

For an assessment measurement tool to be effective, your faculty colleagues have to be interested in the results and see those results as telling them something meaningful about student learning in your program. Part of this property is gained from having well-designed tools (i.e., tools that have as many of the properties of good assessment measures as possible) and part is from the process by which you conduct your assessment. You can increase interest in assessment measurement by engaging your colleagues in as many steps as possible in the assessment process. By helping to select the outcome to focus on, choosing where to measure learning, designing the measurement tool itself, or helping to score student work with that measurement tool, your colleagues will tend to be interested in the measurement and see meaning in the findings.

Convergence

While it is perfectly acceptable to use a single measurement tool to assess your student learning outcome, we find that using a combination of complementary measurement tools provides a richer, more nuanced understanding of student learning. One common approach to this is to look at a direct measurement of student learning, like rubric scores or exam item scores, alongside an indirect measurement of student learning, like survey item responses (more on the terms *direct* and *indirect* later).

For example, let's say you applied a rubric to student presentations and found that students did a really great job organizing their content and constructing an argument, but their use of supportive visual aids and their delivery techniques were surprisingly poor. In addition, let's say you asked students in a survey about their learning experiences related to giving a presentation and found that the majority of students said the way that they learned to give a presentation was by figuring it out on their own. Surprisingly, very few of your students reported ever receiving any formal instruction on presentation skills. Taken together, these findings identify a problem in student learning (i.e., they are weak at delivering a presentation) and point you toward at least one solution (e.g., add instruction on giving a presentation to your curriculum).

Categories to Consider

Every assessment measurement tool can be categorized as either direct or indirect. This major categorization is very important when deciding which assessment measures to choose. Beyond being considered direct or indirect, we can categorize assessment measurement tools by where they are administered and developed.

Direct Measures

These measurement tools involve looking at something students have done that directly demonstrates their learning. Primarily, direct measures involve exams and rubric evaluation of student work or performances. In general, in order to understand student accomplishment of a learning outcome, you need to use at least one direct measurement.

Indirect Measures

These measurement tools capture students' perceptions of their learning and the educational environment that supports learning. In other words, these measures indirectly tell you about student learning. While surveys are the most commonly used indirect assessment measurement tools, both interviews and focus groups are also useful indirect ways to measure learning. Indirect measurements are a good supplement to direct measures that can enhance understanding of patterns of learning seen through direct measurement and can increase the ability to take targeted actions for improvement.

Where Assessment Measurement Occurs

Both direct and indirect assessment can be embedded into a course or be something that happens outside of the formal curriculum. Embedded measurement requires collecting an assignment or exam responses from within a course and then looking at that evidence in light of the program learning outcome. Something to keep in mind when selecting an embedded assignment or exam is that it needs to be designed to reflect learning that goes beyond the specific content of the course it will be collected from. For example, let's say you have decided to collect a lab report from a senior-level chemistry course. The focus of the assignment might be on things like getting the data and analyses correct, but because it also asks students to describe their methodology in detail, the assignment could be used to understand achievement of your outcome about following scientific procedures.

There are several benefits to embedded measurement, including that because the assignment or exam is already in place faculty do not have to spend a lot of time developing it. Instead, faculty can focus efforts on possible modifications to the existing exam or assignment and the development of a rubric or scoring guide that focuses on learning related to the program outcome. As a bonus, students tend to be motivated to do their best work because the embedded assessment counts toward their grade; seeing students' best can help you to feel confident you are developing a clear understanding of learning outcome achievement.

We like to call assessment activities that happen outside of the formal curriculum *add-on assessment*. These are additional tasks that ask students to do something beyond their required course work. Beyond surveys, the most commonly used add-ons that we see are standardized exams. The immediate appeal of these for faculty is that you do not have to spend time developing them. A potential drawback is that, as these are done outside of class time and typically do not count for a grade, it can be difficult to motivate students to do their best. We talk later about the pros and cons of using such exams in the section on using published exams.

Where Assessment Measurements Are Developed

Another way to think about both direct and indirect assessments is by where they are developed. An assessment measurement tool that is developed in-house is one that you and your colleagues develop for use in your program. While such tools can require some labor to develop, they are specifically designed to provide actionable information about your program learning outcomes. This means that you will glean a great deal of useful information from them. Externally developed measurement tools, in contrast, are developed and ready to use, which saves time; however, they tend to be financially costly and, because they were not developed specifically for your learning outcomes, there is no guarantee that you will be able to use all (or even most) of the data you get from using the tool.

A Few Considerations for Choosing Specific Types of Assessment Measures

As we said earlier, no single measurement tool is perfect; the trick is to find the one that works best for you. While there are many different ways to go about measuring student learning for assessment purposes, we are focusing here on five of the most common approaches. For each we'll share a few thoughts about when it might be the most appropriate tool and consider the pros and cons of using it. A summary of the pros and cons for each type is presented in Table 6.1.

TABLE 6.1

Overview of Advantages and Disadvantages of Different Approaches to Measuring Student Learning for Program Assessment

PROS	CONS
RUBRIC EVALUATION OF STUDENT WORK	
• Direct observation of student performance • Data collection unobtrusive to students • Students are motivated to do well • Increased likelihood of faculty buy-in	• Takes time and effort to develop rubric • Takes time and effort to apply rubric to student work • Takes time and effort to analyze results • External comparisons not available
IN-HOUSE EXAMS	
• Direct observation of student performance • Aligned with program learning outcomes • If embedded in courses, student motivation is higher • Increased likelihood of faculty buy-in	• Takes time and effort to develop exam • Takes time and effort to score exams • Takes time and effort to analyze results • External comparisons not available
PUBLISHED EXAMS	
• Direct observation of student performance • Reliability and validity are established • External comparisons are available	• May not align with program learning outcomes • May be difficult to motivate students to perform at best level • Sometimes only taken by a select sample of students (i.e., results may not apply to all students) • Often focus more on content knowledge than higher order skills • Can be expensive

(Continues)

TABLE 6.1 *(Continued)*

PROS	CONS
IN-HOUSE SURVEYS	
• Easy to implement • Easy to align with program learning outcomes • Can assess multiple outcomes in one survey • Good supplement to direct measures	• Indirect measure; should not be used alone • External comparisons not available • Takes time and effort to develop • Takes time and effort to analyze responses • Not all students may respond
PUBLISHED SURVEYS	
• Easy to implement • External comparisons available • Can assess multiple outcomes in one survey • Statistical summaries usually done for you • Good supplement to direct measures	• Indirect measure; should not be used alone • May not align with program learning outcomes • Must obtain high response rate in order to use for program-level assessment

Note: With thanks to Allen (2008).

Rubric Evaluation of Student Work

Using rubrics to evaluate student work or performance is a very powerful and versatile approach to program assessment. You can use a rubric as part of your plan to assess just about any outcome, although rubrics are particularly appropriate for when you are looking at anything a student has written, spoken, or produced that did not have a single clear, correct answer. Instructions for how to create and apply a rubric are presented in module 7.

Applying a rubric to student work is sometimes referred to as being an essential part of the process of *performance assessment* or *authentic assessment*. These terms mean that you are asking students to demonstrate student learning outcome–related knowledge or skills in a way that reflects the outcome and your discipline in a real way. In other words, if your outcome states that students will be able to critically evaluate source material to construct an argument, authentic assessment would involve having students engage in this activity and then looking at what they produce with a rubric. It would not be considered authentic assessment to ask students to take a multiple-choice exam with items asking about the process of evaluating source material or using it to construct an argument. It has been our experience that faculty tend to pay more attention to results of authentic assessments and are thus more likely to act on them.

A major value of a rubric is that because it is designed to look at an outcome in terms of specific skills and components, applying it results in information about each of those skills and components. In addition, the descriptions for each level of performance provide you with an understanding of the level of student accomplishment of each skill and component. These things make the evidence you generate from your rubric highly actionable.

A clear advantage of using rubrics is that you tend to get good faculty buy-in, especially if you have involved your faculty colleagues in the creation and application of the rubrics. In addition, as students are submitting the work as part of a graded course experience, they tend to be motivated to perform at their best. Looking at your students' best efforts will ensure that you are reaching a good understanding of what your students are capable of.

The potential challenges of using rubrics mostly involve the time and effort required to develop them, apply them, and analyze the results. The required time and effort tend to be greater the first time you use a rubric and become less and less of a demand as you become more experienced with rubrics—something to keep in mind if the work involved feels too great the first time around.

The other challenge with using a rubric, or really any assessment measurement tool that you have developed in-house, is that external comparison data are not available. Without an external group to compare yourself to, you must set an internal criterion for success. For example, you might establish that you expect the majority of the scores on your rubric to be at the highest level. This self-set criterion can serve as a starting point for discussing whether or not your students have successfully demonstrated the outcome.

In-House Exams

As the name implies, these are exams that are created by faculty within your program. Although an assessment exam could be embedded within a course and even count toward a course grade, there are some important features and characteristics of exams that are created for assessment purposes. One of these key things is that when using an exam for assessment the focus is on each exam item, not overall exam performance. Each item is written to measure accomplishment of a unique component of the learning outcome you are assessing. By focusing on performance on each item aggregated across students, you develop a clear picture of what it is that students have learned and what needs improvement. The process of developing an exam for program assessment purposes is explained in detail in module 8. "Exams: Asking Questions That Provide the Answers You Need."

A clear benefit of developing your own exams is that you are able to make sure that each item will tell you something relevant and actionable. If you involve multiple faculty in the process of development, there is an increased likelihood of faculty buy-in to the assessment process. In addition, if the exam is embedded into a course, then students will tend to perform at their best, giving you a clear picture of what they have learned.

A drawback of using an in-house exam is that developing and scoring your own exam takes time and effort. Of course, you may become more efficient with these processes as you gain experience. As with other assessment measurement tools that are developed in-house, there are no available comparison data. This means that you, as a faculty, will need to establish your own criterion for success. For example, you might decide that 75% of students must answer an item correctly in order to consider that particular component successfully demonstrated.

Published Exams

Although they are often referred to as standardized exams, we prefer to call them published exams to indicate that they are developed by a third party outside of your institution. There is a wide array of published exams that could be used for assessment purposes in higher education, including licensing or certification exams, exams used in graduate admissions, subject-specific exams, as well as exams that test specific skills.

As with other direct measures, published exams involve observation of students' actual performance, which enhances validity. There are also some unique advantages of published exams. An obvious advantage is that they already exist; that is, you don't have to create them. An additional advantage is that they have already gone through some type of evaluation of their reliability and validity. Finally, a feature that many people find attractive is the availability of norms or comparison scores so they can gauge how well their students perform compared to those at other institutions.

Although there are certainly situations in which it makes sense to use a published exam, these types of measures are not without their disadvantages. One of the biggest disadvantages actually stems from one of the advantages, namely, the fact that you did not create it. As a result, it is sometimes hard to know exactly what the exam is measuring and if it aligns with your program's outcomes and curriculum. A related challenge occurs if the publisher provides only total scores or subscores related to specific content areas. Both of these limit how actionable the results are. Another challenge is student motivation. These exams are usually administered outside of a normal classroom or program setting, and when there is no grade at stake, it can be difficult to motivate students to show up for the exam and perform at their best level. Some of these exams do have some stakes attached, such as graduate admission exams or licensure exams; however, that leads to another possible disadvantage, namely that only some of your students will take the exam. If only students applying to graduate school take the exam then it's hard to know how your students perform overall. Yet another possible drawback is that many of these exams focus on content knowledge rather than higher order skills. Finally, some published exams are quite expensive, and most program budgets can't absorb the cost.

Given the considerable number of drawbacks to using published exams, you might ask whether it is ever appropriate to use them. Here are some guidelines for deciding whether a specific published exam will meet your needs. First, investigate whether you can get a sample of the exam and compare the content that's covered by the exam questions to your program curriculum and learning outcomes to see how closely they are aligned. Second, find out in what form the results are provided. Ideally you will be able to see scores for each item; however, it can also be desirable if the publisher provides scores on subscales related to specific content areas. The ability to gauge level of student learning in specific areas makes it easier to take action on the results. In general, we have found that exams designed explicitly for assessment purposes tend to be more likely to meet these conditions than exams designed for other purposes, such as predicting performance in graduate programs.

If you do decide to use a published exam, you can work to increase student motivation to perform on the exam by connecting exam scores to a course or program requirement. For example, you could make passing the exam with a minimum score a graduation requirement. This would encourage students to study and prepare for the exam, which would result in exam data that reflect what your students have learned and what needs improvement.

In-House Surveys

When you want to know what students believe they have learned, understand the kinds of learning behaviors they have engaged in, or their thoughts about how your program's curriculum has contributed to their learning, then a survey is most likely the assessment tool you want to use. As noted earlier, surveys do not provide direct evidence of student learning, but rather provide student opinions about their learning and experiences. Thus, you would not want a survey to be your only measure of your outcomes. Instead, you'll want to use a survey as a supplement to a more direct measure of learning. For more on how to design a survey for assessment purposes, see module 9, "Surveys: Finding Out What Your Students Think."

A major benefit of using in-house surveys is that you can design a single survey to gather information about all of your student learning outcomes. As with exams, the key to actionable responses is to design the survey so that each item tells you something unique about student learning. Surveys tend to be easy to implement, especially with the availability of online survey tools.

However, because surveys are easy to implement, students tend to receive a lot of survey invitations, reducing the likelihood that they will notice and respond to any particular online survey invitation. Fortunately, there are strategies (discussed in module 9) to increase the likelihood that your students will respond to your request. Other drawbacks of in-house surveys are that it takes time to develop and analyze them and that there are no comparison data available.

Published Surveys

There are a few national published surveys that could be used as part of an assessment plan. Notable examples include the National Survey of Student Engagement (NSSE, 2013) published by the NSSE Institute at Indiana University, as well as the College Senior Survey published by the Higher Education Research Institute (Cooperative Institutional Research Program, 2016) at UCLA. Both surveys include a wide variety of questions about students' attitudes, level of satisfaction, behaviors, and perceptions of their abilities and experiences. Although many of the items are not related to student learning, both surveys include a substantial number of items that are related to knowledge and skills, as well as experiences that might contribute to their learning. The types of knowledge and skills covered by those items are not specific to any particular disciplinary program; however, they are knowledge and skills that many disciplines, and higher education in general, find valuable, such as writing, oral communication, problem-solving, understanding other people, and leadership.

Published surveys offer several advantages. First, they already exist so you don't have to take the time to create a survey, and someone else has already established their reliability and validity. Second, they are relatively easy to implement (with some caveats). Some of them also allow you to gauge student development over time. Third, a large advantage to published surveys over in-house surveys is the availability of comparator data, either from a national sample or from institutions that have some similarities with yours.

Using published student surveys for program-level assessment poses some distinct challenges. As noted previously, the types of knowledge and skills covered by these surveys are not specific to any particular disciplinary program, so it can be challenging to tie the results back to your outcomes and your curriculum to recommend actions for improvement. Another challenge is that it is essential to achieve a high response rate in order for there to be enough of your majors in the overall sample to be meaningful. For example, a 30% response rate might be fine at the institutional level, but if you are not one of the larger major programs, there is a chance that there could be very few of your majors in the sample that responded. In general, published surveys are better for institution-level assessment rather than program-level assessment.

Summary

There are three major types of assessment measurement tools: rubrics, exams, and surveys. Many factors must be considered when deciding what types of measurement tools to use, including the language of your outcome, existing evidence of student learning, and even the time and effort required to develop or use the tool. Utilizing more than one tool, such as a set of exam items and a set of survey items, will help you to develop a rich, clear picture of student learning. Instructions for how to develop and use each of the three major types of assessment measurement tools follow in the next three modules (modules 7–9).

7

RUBRICS

Creating and Using Rubrics for Program Assessment

Rubrics may be the single most powerful and versatile assessment measurement tool your program can utilize for assessment. You can use a rubric as part of your plan to assess any outcome, and rubrics are essential whenever you are looking at anything a student has written, spoken, or produced that did not have a single clear, correct answer. A rubric is the key to unlocking the evidence of student learning outcome achievement from the student work you are examining.

As described in module 6, "Assessment Measurement Tools: Determining What Your Students Are Learning," applying a rubric to student work is sometimes described as being an essential part of the process of *performance assessment* or *authentic assessment.* These terms mean that you are applying your rubric to work that asks students to demonstrate student learning outcome–related knowledge or skills in a way that reflects the outcome and your discipline in a real way. For example, if your outcome is that students are able to apply the theories of your discipline to real-world situations, then an authentic assessment would involve asking them to do just that, such as through completing a service-learning experience and then writing a paper connecting their experience to theory. You would then apply a rubric to those papers to understand achievement of the student learning outcome. If instead you asked students to identify examples of theory application in a multiple-choice exam, then the assessment would not be considered performance-based or "authentic" because students would not be performing the skill nor would they be engaging in an authentic demonstration of the outcome.

In this module we'll define exactly what a *rubric* is, go through the steps for creating a rubric, and share a few considerations for using rubrics for assessment. You can find examples of rubrics in Tables 7.1 through 7.4.

What Is a Rubric?

A rubric is a guide for evaluating student work along identified dimensions. The dimensions are specific skills or components of the student learning outcome you are assessing. For each dimension there are concrete descriptors for different levels of performance. Essentially, a rubric spells out your professional judgments about expected qualities of student work and aligns them with a rating scale.

A major value of a rubric is that because it is designed to look at an outcome in terms of specific skills and components, applying it results in information about each of those skills and components. In addition, the descriptions for each level of performance provide you with an understanding of how well your students are achieving each skill and component. These things make the evidence you generate from your rubric highly actionable. You will develop an understanding of which dimensions students are successfully demonstrating, which may need targeted improvement, and even a sense of where students currently are in their skill set so that you can work to improve from that point. For example, let's say you used the rubric in Table 7.1 to look at five dimensions of written communication skills. By applying the rubric to papers written by students in your program, you find that your students are demonstrating strong skills when it comes to mechanics, style, the use of thesis statements, and the ability to organize ideas in their papers, but they are not doing so well when it comes to supporting their ideas with evidence. For this skill you can see that the majority of your students are at the "Developing (2)" level of your four-point rubric. By looking at the description in that cell of the rubric, you will understand that this means the majority of your students are including evidence in their papers but are not making clear connections between that evidence and the points they are trying to support; essentially, they seem to be making the mistake of assuming that the evidence speaks for itself and there is no clear need to connect it to their argument. This provides you with an identified starting point for discussing the types of actions for improvement you need to implement. As you can imagine, this type of rubric-evidence-driven conversation is much more productive and beneficial than just discussing an overall sense that students don't write as well as you might like.

As you can see in Table 7.1, a rubric takes the form of a table or grid. The columns represent the ordered levels of performance, while the rows represent the different skills or components of the outcome that you are assessing. Generally there are three, four, or five levels of performance described, while the number of rows depends on the outcome you are working to understand student achievement of and the student work you will apply it to. Within

TABLE 7.1

Written Communication Rubric With Five Components and Four Levels Of Performance

Component	Accomplished (4)	Proficient (3)	Developing (2)	Novice (1)
Style	Uses words with precise meaning and an appropriate level of specificity. Sentences are varied yet clearly structured and carefully focused, not long and rambling.	Primarily uses words accurately and effectively. Sentences are primarily clear, well structured, and focused, though some may be awkward or ineffective.	Word choice is sometimes vague, imprecise, or inappropriate. Sentence structure is generally correct, but sentences may be wordy, unfocused, repetitive, or confusing.	Misuses words; employs inappropriate language. Contains many awkward sentences; sentence structure is simple or monotonous.
Mechanics	Almost entirely free of spelling, punctuation, and grammatical errors.	May contain some errors, which may annoy the reader but not impede understanding.	Contains several mechanical errors, which may temporarily confuse the reader but not impede overall understanding.	Contains either many mechanical errors or a few important errors that block the reader's understanding and ability to see connection between thoughts.
Thesis Statement	Thesis statement is clearly communicated, worth developing, and engaging.	Presents a thesis statement that can be developed.	Presents thesis statement that is weak, or too broad to be developed.	Attempted thesis statement lacks clarity.
Organization	Uses a logical structure appropriate to paper's subject, purpose, and audience. Sophisticated transitional sentences often develop one idea from the previous one or identify their logical relations. It guides the reader through the chain of reasoning or progression of ideas.	Shows a progression of ideas and uses fairly sophisticated transitional devices (e.g., may move from least to most important idea).	May list ideas or arrange them randomly rather than using any evident structure. May use transitions, but they are likely to be sequential (first, second, third) rather than logic based.	May have random organization, lacking internal paragraph coherence and using few or inappropriate transitions.
Supporting Evidence	Uses appropriate, relevant, and compelling content to support ideas, convey understanding of the topic, and shape the whole work.	Content is appropriate and relevant so that ideas are supported sufficiently. Work is generally shaped through support.	Demonstrates use of supportive content but assumes that supportive content speaks for itself and needs no application to the point being discussed, or inconsistently supports ideas with content.	Often uses ineffective or inappropriate content (e.g., opinions, examples, or clichés) to support points, or offers little evidence of any kind.

Note. Some language in the rubric was taken from the Written Communication VALUE Rubric (Rhodes, 2010).

each cell of the table are descriptions of the qualities of student work for that component at that performance level.

Let's look at the example rubric in Table 7.2. This example comes from a liberal studies program that prepares students to become teachers. The outcome being assessed is "Liberal Studies students will professionally communicate assessment results to relevant constituencies." The rubric will be applied to letters that students write to parents about their child's standardized test scores. In this example, there are five defined levels of performance, ranging from *Excellent* (5) to *Unacceptable* (1). Three components are included in the rubric: the use of Professional Writing, the Explanation of Scores provided, and the sense of Perspective that students provide in their letters. If you read the detailed descriptions across each of the rows you'll see that the described performance moves from the ideal (under *Excellent*) to the very poor (under *Unacceptable*). What you'll also notice is that the same elements are described in each cell across a row. For example, across the Professional Writing row you'll see that tone, message, and errors occur in every cell. This consistency is important for applying the rubric. If the cells across a row have different things included in them it becomes possible for a student to demonstrate elements that are represented in more than one level, making it very difficult to decide upon a performance level for that student.

Five Steps to Creating a Rubric

Once you've selected a learning outcome to work on, there are five steps to creating a rubric to assess it. While you can certainly carry these out on your own, it is optimal to work with a partner or a small committee to complete the five steps. This is because rubrics created by a group tend to capture more of the agreed-on ideas and be richer as a result. Working on a rubric with others starts a conversation about what it is that you value and how your program is helping students to achieve those things. The process of writing down your criteria and your standards for the outcome on which you are focusing helps you to clarify what you mean by success and what you intend your students to accomplish. For example, we often use terms like *critical thinking* or *cultural sensitivity* in our student learning outcomes, and just as often individual faculty members will have different conceptions of what these terms mean. The process of developing a rubric together will help you to develop a shared understanding among program faculty that you can then express to your students. In fact, we recommend sharing the rubric with your students, such as by using it in courses with relevant assignments, in order to establish a clear, consistent message about expectations for learning in the program.

TABLE 7.2

Rubric For the Outcome "Liberal Studies students will professionally communicate assessment results to relevant constituencies."

Component	Excellent (5)	Above Average (4)	Average (3)	Below Average (2)	Unacceptable (1)
Professional Writing	Writing is professional in tone and message; it does not use professional jargon nor does it talk down to the audience. No errors in spelling, grammar, or syntax.	Writing is professional in tone and message. One or two errors in spelling, grammar, or syntax.	With few exceptions writing is professional in tone and message. More than two errors in spelling, grammar, or syntax.	Writing is not consistently professional in tone and message. Errors in spelling, grammar, or syntax throughout.	Errors make the letter difficult to read in places, or tone and/or message is not professional.
Explanation of Scores	Scores are correctly explained in simple, clear terms. A clear explanation of the strengths and weaknesses indicated by the scores is given.	With one or two exceptions the scores are clearly and correctly explained. Strengths and weaknesses are indicated.	Most of the scores are explained clearly and correctly. The strengths and weaknesses are not perfectly clear or are not accurately explained.	Some of the scores are explained correctly and clearly. Strengths and weaknesses are not clearly or accurately explained.	Scores are not clearly explained, and/or strengths and weaknesses are not indicated.
Perspective	It is very clear that the test is only one factor in assessing learning. It is explained that other forms of assessment are used. It is clear that multiple assessments are needed to understand learning and success.	It is explained that other assessments are utilized; however, it is not completely clear how those other assessments help create a better understanding of the reported scores.	It is explained that other assessments are utilized; however, the explanation of how they help clarify reported scores is vague.	It is explained that other assessments are utilized, but how they help clarify the reported scores is not explained.	It is not clear that other assessments are utilized. No sense of perspective is given.

Note. The assignment for this was a letter to be written to parents about their child's standardized test scores.

The five steps to creating a rubric for a selected learning outcome are the following:

1. Select the assignment to which you will apply the rubric.
2. Determine the dimensions of the learning outcome.
3. Decide on the number of levels of performance you will include.
4. Write the descriptors for each component of the learning outcome.
5. Test the rubric and use the findings to edit your rubric.

Let's look at each of these steps in more detail and create a sample rubric for the student learning outcome "Students will deliver persuasive oral presentations." This outcome comes from an undergraduate business management program, which has a team of three faculty working together to develop the rubric.

Select the Assignment to Which You Will Apply the Rubric

Knowing which student learning outcome we are creating a rubric for will provide most of the information you need to begin developing your rubric. Another key piece of information comes from the assignment to which you will apply it. There is often more than one way for students to demonstrate outcome achievement, and the way that they are asked (i.e., the assignment) influences which components you include in your rubric and some of the qualities of student work that you will define in your rubric.

In our example, our business management program faculty wanted to understand their students' ability to deliver persuasive oral presentations. Our faculty looked to their curriculum map (see module 4, "Curriculum and Outcome Mapping: Understanding the Path to Student Learning in Your Program") and saw that there were two different senior-level courses where students were expected to master this outcome. In one of those courses the presentation that students give is a five-minute sales pitch. This pitch is to be delivered at a conference table to a small group of faculty without the use of any supportive aids, like notes or visuals. In the other course, students were expected to present a proposed solution to an issue experienced by a nonprofit organization that they had been working with over the course of the semester. Students were asked to give a 20-minute presentation and to support their points with evidence and visual aids. As you can imagine, these two very different presentations would necessitate differences in the rubric for the outcome. The faculty decided to use the longer presentation for their assessment, as they felt it would give students more of a chance to demonstrate the desired skills.

Determine the Dimensions of the Learning Outcome

Next you need to decide what the dimensions of your student learning outcome are, while considering what you expect to be demonstrated in the selected assignment. This step takes a bit of reflection and consideration of the possibilities. You will want to think about what it is you look for when evaluating students on work related to the outcome, as those things are good candidates for rubric components. If you need more ideas, it can help to look at existing rubrics to see what components other faculty have included in rubrics for similar outcomes. You can ask colleagues in your program, as well as in other programs at your institution, to share examples and look online for more. There are a great many rubrics available on the Internet that can be found by searching for the word *rubric* and a key word or phrase from your outcome (e.g., *written communication, ethical reasoning, creative thinking*). When searching for rubrics online, it can sometimes help to limit your search to those sites ending in *.edu* so that you are looking only at rubrics from colleges and universities. Another great source of example rubrics is the Association of American Colleges & Universities' (AAC&U) set of VALUE rubrics (Rhodes, 2010). Each of the 16 VALUE rubrics is available on the AAC&U website to download for free.

Once you have a list of possible components, you'll want to select the ones to include in your rubric that seem essential for understanding achievement of your outcome. It is important to note that there is not a required number of components or a limit on the possible number that you can include in your rubric. The key is that you end up with a rubric that captures what you consider important for students to be able to demonstrate. You'll also want to make sure that there is no overlap in the components you include. For example, it would not make sense to have a rubric component for the overall quality of writing and also have components for syntax, for grammar, and for word choice. Each component should tell you something unique, so in this example you'd either want to cut the overall quality component or cut the syntax, grammar, and word-choice components.

Our business management program faculty began by brainstorming their own lists of possible components and then reviewed existing rubrics for both *persuasive communication* and the broader category of *oral communication*. After discussing what was essential for students to be able to demonstrate for this outcome in their 20-minute presentations addressing an issue of the nonprofit organization they have been working with, the faculty decided to include components for delivery of the presentation, connection with the audience, overall organization of the presentation, and the use of visual support.

Decide on the Number of Levels of Performance You Will Include

The number of levels of performance you choose is up to you. That said, rubrics commonly include between three (e.g., weak, satisfactory, strong) and five (e.g., unacceptable, marginal, acceptable, good, outstanding) categories of performance. The reason for this is that you certainly want more than two levels of performance, because two would equate to a pass/fail rating. A pass/fail rating would not do a very good job of meaningfully differentiating student performances or likely produce information that is highly actionable. However, more than five levels starts to require writing descriptions for each level that have very small difference between them, which could make the rubric difficult to create and later to apply. If you are uncertain about how many levels to include, we recommend that you start with a plan to include four. As you work through the next step, writing your descriptors, you should be able to easily adjust the number of levels up or down from there if it seems like that is what you need in order to capture the essential information.

When you look at most completed rubrics you'll notice that the levels of performance are generally given a descriptor, a number, or both. We tend to like using both. The reasons for this preference have to do with the process of applying the rubric to student work and, later, the process of analyzing the data. We find that a descriptive word used to label each performance level can help to guide your attention toward the right cells of the table when you are applying the rubric. A number, in contrast, gives you something simple and brief to record as you score and, later, can be used to generate basic descriptive statistics. A general rule when using numbers to label your rubric components is that the lowest performance level of your rubric is assigned a number 1, with each level up the performance scale increasing in numerical value from there. This way greater average scores indicate higher levels of performance on the rubric.

The left-to-right ordering of the levels of performance on your rubric can be either from high to low or from low to high. The ordering is really determined by personal preference. We tend to like the high-to-low presentation, as we find that it is easiest for us to approach student work with the highest performance ideal as a starting point (on the left) and then work down from there (reading left to right). We have worked with many faculty who prefer the low-to-high approach as they like to start by reading the lowest performance description and working their way up from that point.

The business management program faculty decided to include four levels of performance in their rubric. They chose to label each level of performance with both a word and a number. Those labels, from left to right on their rubric, are Superior (4), Good (3), Adequate (2), and Inadequate (1).

Write the Descriptors for Each Component of the Learning Outcome

After you've determined the specific components to include in your rubric, you need to create descriptors for each. There are three steps to writing these descriptors:

1. Describe the best possible work for each component. This is the easiest way to get started. You know what an excellent demonstration of the component would look like. It's the "A" work that you hope to see. Define that for each component. If you are struggling to get started, check out what those sample rubrics you gathered include. There may be language in those examples that will help you to find your own descriptions.

2. Describe unacceptable work. The next easiest thing to do is to define the other end of the spectrum. Assuming the student turned something in, what does unacceptable look like? Define this for each component. You should note that this is different from the student not doing the work. A student who does not demonstrate a particular component of the rubric in the work he or she produces can be assigned a zero, or no score, on that component. For example, if a component of the rubric looks at the bibliography for a paper, but the student did not include a bibliography, then he or she would not have demonstrated even the lowest level of work that is described on the rubric.

3. Describe the intermediate levels of work. Now that you have your upper and lower anchors, it's time to define the levels in the middle. Each level should be a meaningful step away from the level next to it. As we stated earlier, it is also important that for each particular component the same elements are included in each performance level of the rubric. This consistency is important for the rubric application process. When the levels are inconsistent you might find that a student demonstrates things that are described in more than one level, making it impossible to assign a single score for that rubric component.

Our business management program faculty found that the VALUE rubric for oral communication included language that they found very helpful in defining the levels of performance, so they decided to include language from that rubric in creating their own rubric (Rhodes, 2010). The draft rubric that they created is in Table 7.3.

TABLE 7.3

Draft of a Rubric For the Outcome "Students will deliver persuasive oral presentations."

Outcome Component	Superior (4)	Good (3)	Adequate (2)	Inadequate (1)
Delivery	Delivery techniques (posture, gesture, eye contact, and vocal expressiveness) make the presentation compelling. Speaker appears polished and confident in giving presentation and answering questions.	Delivery techniques (posture, gesture, eye contact, and vocal expressiveness) make the presentation interesting. Speaker appears comfortable in giving presentation and/or answering questions.	Delivery techniques (posture, gesture, eye contact, and vocal expressiveness) make the presentation understandable. Speaker appears tentative in giving presentation and/or answering questions.	Delivery techniques (posture, gesture, eye contact, and vocal expressiveness) detract from the understandability of the presentation. Speaker appears uncomfortable in giving presentation and/or answering questions.
Connection With Audience	Topic and language choices in each presentation are **purposefully tailored** to the audience's needs and expectations for the message and the occasion.	Topic and language choices in each presentation are **fully appropriate** to the audience's needs and expectations for the message and the occasion.	Topic and language choices in each presentation are somewhat appropriate to the audience's needs and expectations for the message and the occasion.	Topic and language choices in each presentation are rarely appropriate to the audience's needs and expectations for the message and the occasion.
Overall Organization	Organizational pattern is clearly and consistently observable, is skillful, and makes the content of the presentation cohesive.	Organizational pattern is clearly and consistently observable within the presentation.	Organizational pattern is intermittently observable within the presentation.	Organizational pattern is not observable within the presentation.
Visual Support	Visual aids enhance the presentation. They are prepared in a professional manner. Font on visuals is large enough to be seen by all. Information is organized to maximize audience understanding. Details are minimized so that main points stand out.	Visual aids contribute to the quality of the presentation. Font size is appropriate for reading. Appropriate information is included. Some material is not supported by visual aids.	Visual aids are poorly prepared or used inappropriately. Font is too small to be easily seen. Too much information is included. Unimportant material is highlighted. Listeners may be confused.	Visual aids are so poorly prepared that they detract from the presentation.

Note. In this draft, the faculty member who tested the rubric struggled with language in the "Connection With Audience" component. Specifically it was not clear how to differentiate the phrase "purposely tailored" in the superior level from the phrase "fully appropriate" in the good level. Some components of the rubric come from the Oral Communication VALUE Rubric (Rhodes, 2010).

Test the Rubric and Use the Findings to Edit Your Rubric

After you have a draft of your rubric, we recommend that you test it out on a few examples of student work before you use it for assessment. This testing process will help to ensure that you have created a clearly written rubric that can be applied to student work in a consistent manner. It is best to ask a colleague who was not involved in the development of the rubric to do this test for you. This is because those faculty who were involved in developing the rubric know exactly what each cell of the rubric is intended to mean and will not have an easy time identifying places where the rubric may lack clarity. The test of the rubric should involve a check for the clarity of the content of the rubric and consider whether the rubric dimensions capture what is essential for students to demonstrate their achievement of the outcome.

If the test of the rubric identifies issues with the rubric, then you'll want to correct those before you formally apply the rubric as part of your assessment plan. If the changes are minor, such as editing a few words, make the changes and then run them by the colleague who tested the rubric to see if the changes fix the issue. When you agree that the issue has been resolved, then proceed with your assessment plan. If the changes your rubric needs are major, such as having to add a new element or increase the number of levels of performance, then you'll want to test the revised rubric before you finalize it and move forward with your assessment plan.

Whatever you do, do not get stuck in an endless cycle of test-edit-test; after all, your goal is not to develop the perfect rubric, but to understand and improve student learning. It may help to remember that no assessment measurement tool is perfect (see module 6, "Assessment Measurement Tools: Determining What Your Students Are Learning"). You need to get your rubric to a point that it contains the dimensions you consider essential and clear descriptors and then move forward with your assessment plan. Very often rubrics get a bit of further editing during the process of applying them to student work or get further editing after the assessment cycle is complete. Realistically, it may take several assessment cycles for you to get to a rubric that you feel is as perfect as possible.

Our team from the business management program asked a colleague who was not a part of their development team to test their rubric draft, which is shown in Table 7.3. They provided their colleague with recordings of three student presentations given in a prior semester. That colleague found that most of the rubric was clear and easy to apply but struggled with part of the "Connection With Audience" component. Specifically, it was unclear how to differentiate the phrase "purposely tailored," in the Superior level, from the phrase "fully appropriate," in the Good level, when describing a student's topic and language choices. The colleague felt that it was impossible to really know the process by which a student presenter had chosen his or her topic and language (i.e., was it on purpose or did it just happen?), but that it was always clear if the topic and language choices were appropriate. As such, the rubric development team edited the descriptors used and checked the new descriptors with their colleague, which resolved the issue and allowed them to move forward with applying the rubric.

Applying Your Rubric

Just like when developing the rubric, the process of applying the rubric is best completed as a group activity. In addition to the meaningful discussions that the process generates about your students' knowledge and abilities, applying the rubric with a partner or small committee can help to ensure an agreed-on usage of the rubric and thus increase interrater reliability.

The process of coming to an agreed-on usage of the rubric is called *norming*. The norming process involves having all of the faculty participants independently apply the rubric to the same example of student work and then discuss the scores they assigned for each dimension. The purpose of that discussion is to understand similarities and differences of opinion in the scores given and, ultimately, to come to agreement about the proper scores to assign. This process of applying the rubric, discussing scores, and working toward agreement typically takes multiple rounds. However, even if you find that you agree entirely on the very first round, we think it is a good idea to go through the norming process at least one more time to make sure that you continue to agree and to further familiarize yourself with the rubric. By the time norming is complete, everyone involved should feel very familiar with the rubric and feel confident that he or she can apply the rubric in a way that is consistent with how the others involved would apply it.

When the norming process is complete and it is time to apply the rubric, while not required, it can be a good idea to have each example of student work scored independently by two faculty. This will allow you to check that you have in fact consistently scored the work. When a difference in scores appears, you can either have a conversation about why you differed and come to an agreed-on score or ask a third faculty member to apply the rubric and resolve the difference. This process of double scoring each example of student work can assure your colleagues that the rubric application process was done reliably and fairly.

Another way to help increase fairness in applying the rubric is by redacting student names from student work prior to providing that work to the faculty who will apply the rubric. By not knowing whose work is being evaluated, faculty are able to avoid the possibility that previous experiences with the student may influence the scores they assign. If the student work that will be scored with the rubric comes from more than one course, or section of a course, then it may make sense to also redact the faculty member's name from the student assignments. This can help to assure those colleagues that you were not considering their individual course content, teaching style, or personality when scoring student work from their courses. If you do redact names from the work being examined, then you will want to assign each piece of student work a code. This way you can connect the scores back to the artifact they were assigned to; compare the scores assigned by different readers; and, if desired, keep a list of which code you assigned to which student so that you can ultimately connect back to the name of the student who submitted the work.

There are two basic approaches to record the scores that you assign as you apply the rubric. The first approach is to make a copy of the rubric for each example of student work you will score. As you score the work, you would then circle, or otherwise mark, the rubric to indicate which scores you are assigning to it. You will also want to be sure to record the student name or code on the rubric so that you can connect your scores back to the student work. An example of this is shown in Table 7.4. This process works very well; however, a downside is that you will use at least one full sheet of paper for each artifact you examine.

The second approach is to generate a score sheet that allows you to record your student names or codes, scores, and comments about those scores. An example of a score sheet is shown in Figure 7.1. As a score sheet does not take up a full sheet of paper, you can print multiple score sheets onto a single page, which reduces paper usage and can later make the process of entering scores into a spreadsheet faster (see module 10, "Organizing, Summarizing, and Presenting Your Evidence: Using Microsoft Excel to Make Sense of Your Data").

A Few Things to Consider When Using Rubrics for Assessment

When you plan to incorporate a rubric into your assessment plan (see module 5, "Planning: Creating a Meaningful and Manageable Assessment Plan for Your Program"), there are just a few things you'll want to consider. First, if you've ever used a rubric for grading student work, you should understand that the process of using a rubric for assessment of a learning outcome is slightly different. When grading, you use your rubric to come up with a single score for each student. When using a rubric for assessment you will want separate scores for each dimension of the rubric that are later aggregated across all students. For example, if you were using the rubric shown in Figure 7.4, you'd want to know the number of students who were assigned each of

TABLE 7.4.

Rubric Used as a Score Sheet For the Outcome "Students will be able to identify ethical issues and propose effective approaches to their resolution."

Code:	012			
Component	4. Accomplished	3. Competent	2. Developing	1. Introductory
Ethical Issue Recognition	Student is able to clearly and comprehensively define the ethical issue.	Student is able to define the ethical issue, but definition is unclear or incomplete in some minor aspects.	Student is somewhat able to define the ethical issue, but definition is overly simplistic or incomplete.	Student's attempt to define the ethical issue is incomprehensible.
Proposal of Approach	Student independently and thoughtfully takes a stance on the ethical issue in a logical and powerfully persuasive manner.	Student takes a stance on the ethical issue that is satisfactorily persuasive but lacks clarity or completeness in some minor aspects.	Student takes a stance on the ethical issue, but it is not persuasive, is overly simplistic, and/or is largely unfeasible.	Student does not comprehensibly articulate a stance on the ethical issue.
Implications of Approach	Student thoroughly and clearly articulates wide range of implications of stance, including immediate and/or lasting effects on individuals or groups.	Student articulates implications of stance, including effects on individuals or groups, but scope is limited or description is unclear in some minor aspects.	Student articulates some implications of stance, but discussion of some major effects on individuals or groups is overly simplistic or omitted.	Student does not comprehensibly articulate implications of stance on individuals or groups.
Defense of Approach	Student is able to articulate opposing viewpoints and logically and persuasively defend stance against them.	Student is able to articulate opposing viewpoints and defend stance against them, but defense is not persuasive or logical in some minor aspects.	Student addresses and defends against opposing viewpoints, but defense is not persuasive or logical in key aspects, and/or opposing viewpoints are presented in an overly simplistic manner or are slightly misrepresented.	Student does not engage or address opposing viewpoints at all or does so in an inappropriate or disrespectful manner, and/or key aspects of opposing viewpoints are misrepresented.

Note. This rubric was applied to an assignment that asked students to identify an ethical issue, take a stance on that issue, and defend that stance. The circled descriptors indicate the scores the faculty member who applied the rubric has assigned.

the four performance levels for the "Ethical Issue Recognition" dimension. This would help you understand how well your students are able to demonstrate that component of the outcome being assessed and help you to guide your decisions about needed actions for improvement.

Second, if your assessment plan calls for a student presentation, performance, demonstration, or other "live" activity, you will need to consider whether you want to apply the rubric during that live activity, or whether to record that live activity and apply the rubric at a later time. As we described in module 5, it can be difficult for the faculty member who is teaching the course to apply the rubric while teaching the class. In addition, it is very possible to miss something important during a live performance, whereas with a video record you can back the video up and watch it as many times as you need to fully capture the demonstration of student learning. The video record does not have to be of a professional quality—you can even use a smartphone to record it if that is your only option. If you do choose to apply the rubric during the live demonstration, then consider inviting a faculty member, or even more than one faculty member, who is not teaching the class to apply the rubric.

Figure 7.1. Example of completed rubric score sheets for the rubric shown in Table 7.4.

Paper code: 012		
Outcome element	**Score**	**Comments**
Ethical Issue Recognition	3	Generally good, but not entirely clear why this is a universal issue
Proposal of Approach	3	Stance makes sense, just needs more details for full clarity
Implications of Approach	2	Missing key constituents in consideration of implications
Defense of Approach	1	Only briefly mentions that there are other points of view . . .

Paper code: 013		
Outcome element	**Score**	**Comments**
Ethical Issue Recognition	4	Excellent! Hit all points
Proposal of Approach	3	Very good, just needs more details here
Implications of Approach	4	Well thought out
Defense of Approach	2	Highly oversimplified—needs to think this through more

Third, if you have a large number of students in the courses from which you are collecting student work, consider that you might want to apply the rubric only to a sample of the student work collected. Evaluating a subset of the collected work may be more feasible in terms of faculty time and would still provide you with meaningful evidence of student learning. If you decide that sampling student work is a good approach for your program, then you want to be sure to draw your sample from the entire pool of available work in such a way that every student has an equal chance of being selected into the sample. This is called random sampling and, in effect, it is like putting every student's name on a slip of paper, putting these in a bag, and then drawing them out one by one. While you could draw your sample in that very low-tech way, you could also use Microsoft Excel to generate your sample. This is done by creating a column of student names (or the codes you have assigned them) and a column of random numbers. You then sort the file by the random numbers, and then select the number of students that you wish to include in your sample starting with the first student on the list and going down the list from there. You can find instructions and even videos online that walk you through how to complete these steps to determine a random sample.

The number of students that you include in your sample is up to you as a program faculty. You have to work together to decide what makes for a meaningful sample size. You could use complex statistics to make this decision, but we recommend that instead you follow a more practical approach. This approach would involve considering how many students you believe are sufficient for providing meaningful evidence and how much time you have to put into the scoring process. There is no universally correct sample size. As with most everything to do with assessment, the answer depends on your needs as a faculty.

Summary

Rubrics are essential to assessment. They can be used as part of your assessment plan for any of your program outcomes and are particularly useful when you are focused on learning that does not have a single correct answer. Rubrics allow you to extract meaningful, actionable information about student learning from work that students have produced. In addition, you can use rubrics to communicate expectations for learning with students and faculty.

8

EXAMS

Asking Questions That Provide the Answers You Need

When you are looking to assess an outcome that specifies students will know dates, events, people, places, or other facts, then you might consider using an exam as part of your assessment plan. Exams are particularly great for testing your students' ability to remember things and, we'll argue, you can construct exam items (even closed-ended ones like multiple-choice questions) that ask students to demonstrate much more complex learning.

The key with using exams for assessment is to focus on individual exam items. Each item will tell you something specific and unique about what students have learned, thus providing you with evidence you can act on. This item-by-item approach is much more effective than considering entire exam scores. Total exam scores provide you with an overall sense of student learning but fail to tell you which components of the outcome students have mastered and which may need some work to improve. In this module, we'll walk you through the steps involved in planning your exam, provide some exam-writing tips, and then share best practices for writing a variety of exam item types.

Planning Your Exam

If you've decided to use an exam to assess one of your student learning outcomes, then the first thing you'll want to do in planning that exam is to examine your curriculum map or outcome map (see module 4, "Curriculum and Outcome Mapping: Understanding the Path to Student Learning in Your Program"). Use your map to determine the senior-most courses in which the outcome is addressed, and then find out if those courses either already incorporate exams or if it is possible to add an exam for program assessment purposes. If a course already includes an exam, you'll want to verify that the faculty member teaching the course is open to possible modifications to that exam so that it captures the information needed for assessment purposes. If the faculty member does not already use an exam in his or her course, then you'll want to make sure not only that the faculty member is okay with adding an exam but also that the exam will count toward the course grade. You want students to do their best on the exam, which they will tend to do if their performance impacts their course grade. If the exam is a nongraded activity, then it can be very difficult to get students to put much effort into preparing for or taking the exam. When this happens, you can't be sure if any poor exam item performance is due to lack of student knowledge on that particular outcome component or an issue with student motivation.

You will want to invite the faculty who will give the exam in their class to participate in its design process. This will help to assure them that the exam will meet their needs for the course and will help you to design an exam that captures essential components of student learning outcome achievement.

Determining what components to ask students about on the exam involves a bit of brainstorming and research. You will want to list out all of those things that students should know if they have accomplished the outcome. To get the most complete list possible, you will want to include multiple faculty in this step. You might also include a review of textbooks, lecture notes, and other instructional materials to help you consider what is taught across your curriculum. The items on your list will serve as the basis of your exam questions, with each item likely representing a single exam question.

Before you start writing exam questions, there are at least three things to consider. First, if you are using an existing exam, you'll want to see which items on your list are already represented on the exam, as you will not need to write questions for those list items. Second, if your list of components to ask about is very long, then you'll likely need to prioritize what you decide to ask about. After all, students will be given some time constraint to complete the exam, whether that will be the length of a typical class meeting or a longer final exam period. You want to consider how many exam items students can be realistically expected to complete in that given time. If you do need to prioritize your list, consider asking some of the items on a midterm while others are asked on the final, or asking students in one section of the course a subset of the items while students in another section are asked a different subset, or even splitting the items across multiple semesters. It is not typically necessary to ask every student every question to determine if students in your program are achieving the outcome. Third, you'll want to think about what kinds of items you want to write, such as essay items or multiple-choice items. We provide considerations and tips for writing a variety of item types later in this module.

As you already know, writing good exam items takes time. You'll want to make sure to allow yourself plenty of time to draft your exam, review it, and finalize it. It can also help to solicit the assistance of multiple colleagues. This will increase the number of good ideas for exam questions, and with multiple faculty dividing and conquering the list of exam items that need to be written, you will be able to draft your exam a bit more quickly.

Once you have a draft of possible items, you'll want to review them and consider testing them out. Ask faculty who were not involved in writing the items to review them, as they will not know exactly what you intended and be more likely than you to see errors or identify when an item is confusing in its phrasing or response options. Faculty reviewers will look for clarity in the questions, consider if closed-ended items (e.g., multiple choice) have a single best answer, and indicate if they believe the level of difficulty is appropriate. If your campus has an assessment office or a center for teaching (or teaching and learning), consider checking with them to see if they offer a professional exam review or other service that might help with the process of finalizing your exams. Finally, you might also consider asking students to try out the items for you. In this case, you'd ask students who are not enrolled in the course to be tested to take the draft exam and share their feedback about the clarity of the items. Timing these students as they take the exam will help you know if the exam is appropriate in length. Obviously, you would ask these students to keep the content of the exam confidential.

If you are not certain you could get students to come in and test your exam, then you might provide a small incentive for their time and effort, like offering pizza during the session. Once you get students to show up you can help to increase the quality of their participation by explaining what you are doing and how you will use the results. We have found that students are generally excited to be included in assessment processes when you explain to them that your goal is to understand student learning and use what you learn to improve your program. It has been our experience that students see assessment as a form of quality assurance for their degree.

After you incorporate suggested changes you will want to give your exam a careful proofread before you finalize it. This may sound obvious, but we want to make sure that you add this step to your to-do list when developing an exam. When it comes to exams, even a minor typo can create confusion in test takers that results in an item having to be thrown out.

Test-Writing Tips

Before we get into tips for writing specific types of exam items, like true-false items, we want to share four general tips for writing your exam that apply regardless of the types of exam items you choose to include. The first is to write exam items that are clear and to the point. This will help students to understand exactly what you are asking so that they can give you their best answer. Items that are written clearly and directly will also help to ensure that you are testing what students know, rather than their ability to keep track of all of the information in a question. As humans we are limited in the amount of information we can keep track of and process at any given time. This limited capacity is a central component of the way our memory system functions (Baddeley & Hitch, 1974). When we load up our system with an attempt to keep track of the numerous details in a complex problem, we tend to have very little capacity left to manipulate that information in order to solve the problem. This is known as cognitive overload (Sweller, 1988). Simple ways to reduce the cognitive load of an exam question include cutting out extraneous details, like unnecessary information or visuals; providing diagrams for spatially organized information; and providing cues or signals that focus attention on necessary information, like the use of bold font to indicate a key word or phrase (Clark, Nguyen, & Sweller, 2006). When you ask faculty and/or students to review your exam items, you can ask them to identify any items that appear to include unnecessary or distracting details and use that feedback to clarify the phrasing of your exam items.

Second, when you are writing your items, especially when you are focusing on writing succinctly, it can become tempting to ask students only for basic recall of information, such as by asking students to provide the date for a particular historical event or to provide the correct term when you give them the definition. This is especially tempting to do when writing closed-ended items like multiple-choice questions. If the learning outcome you are testing specifies that this level of learning (i.e., recognition or recall) is what students need to demonstrate, then this type of item is perfectly appropriate. If, however, you have a learning outcome that specifies students will be able to do something more complex with their learning, such as apply it to new situations or use it to evaluate new information, then you will want to write test items that ask students to do these things. These types of items require what is known as problem-solving transfer (Mayer & Wittrock, 1996). Most of the time, faculty tend to think of this type of transfer test as being limited to open-ended essay questions, but it is not. You can also ask students to demonstrate transfer, or that deeper learning, in closed-ended questions. For example, in a multiple-choice test item you can provide a description of a situation and ask students to identify the theory that is illustrated in the situation. In a label-a-diagram type of item you could provide a diagram of a system students have learned, describe a problem that has occurred in the output of the system, and then ask students to indicate on the diagram what component (or components) of the system are the most likely culprits of the described problem, and even to explain why they believe this to be the case. The point is to not limit yourself to only asking students to demonstrate the most basic levels of learning when you use an exam for assessment.

The third thing to consider when you design your exam is that each item should stand alone. After all, each item should be designed to test a unique component of your student learning outcome. If the items are set up so that the answer to one is the key to answering the next, and so on, then a student who makes an initial mistake will have that mistake perpetuated over the course of all related items. If the exam is graded, then this will unfairly penalize the student repeatedly for the initial error. Beyond that, for your assessment purposes it will become difficult to know if students have not learned a certain component of your learning outcome or if they just made an error on an early item that prevents you from seeing their abilities on subsequent items. If you feel that the only way to design an exam for your outcome is to set it up so that the items build on each other, then consider either setting it up or scoring it a little differently. A modified setup for this type of item is to tell students for each item to assume a specific answer to the previous question (obviously, you would not give them the correct answers). This would guarantee that all of your students would start each problem from the same place so that you could focus on scoring their final answers. Alternatively, modified scoring would require looking at the process followed to solve the problems in addition to whether students get the correct answers. This way you will be able to determine if students are not capable of doing what you ask or if they just made an error somewhere along the way in the exam.

Fourth, it is essential to include simple, succinct directions in your exam. Your directions should indicate how to record answers (e.g., "Using capital letters, write your answer on the line provided"), and whether to show work on problems (e.g., when solving a math problem). If your questions require students to write more than a simple letter when responding, then you might ask them to write neatly. Our favorite instruction on short-answer and essay questions is, "Please write neatly. If I cannot read your answer, I will assume it is wrong." We find that this instruction encourages students to write clearly enough that their answers can be read. In addition, assuming your exam is something students will earn a grade on, your instructions should indicate the point value of each item. On a graded exam, students can use this information to determine which items to focus their efforts on given their time and knowledge constraints. For assessment purposes, you might consider using the point values of items to reflect the importance of tested concepts. For example, if an essay item on your exam is written to capture understanding of an essential major theory, then that item should be worth more points than a true-false item that captures knowledge of a single fact.

If you are going to use multiple types of items on your exam, such as a mixture of multiple-choice, matching, and essay items, then consider grouping those item types into sections and placing instructions at the start of each section. A possible benefit of using multiple item types is that some outcome elements may be best tested using one type of item, such as short answer, while other outcome elements may be best suited to another item type, like multiple-choice questions. In addition, students often feel that they are better at answering one type of item over another, so by including multiple types of items, you are potentially reducing student perception that their abilities relevant to a particular type of test question are influencing their test performance.

Best Practices for Selected-Response Items

Selected-response items are those where students select a response from a set of options. These include multiple-choice items, true-false items, and matching items. These types of items are most commonly used to ask students to demonstrate their mastery of factual information, but they can be used to ask students to demonstrate much more complex thinking. For example, you can give students a set of data and ask them to make inferences about it, provide a problem to solve and ask students to select the correct answer, describe a causal situation and ask students to determine a possible effect, or provide them with a graph and ask them to conclude what it reveals. The limits of selected response items are really up to your imagination and creativity.

A major benefit of using selected-response items is that they can be scored objectively. This can save a lot of time in your assessment process. In fact, if your institution has the resources, you can even use machines to do the scoring. A limitation of selected-response items is that writing them well is not so simple. Here we provide a few guidelines for writing the three major categories of selected-response items.

Multiple Choice

Multiple-choice items include a stem (i.e., the question or incomplete statement) and a set of alternatives (i.e., the response options) to choose from. Good multiple-choice items are generally more difficult to write than other types of test items, as you have to come up with both the stem and a set of plausible alternatives, which takes a bit of time and skill.

When writing the stem for a multiple-choice item, you want to write both concisely and directly, describing a single situation or problem. If you use words like *best* or *sometimes*, then you want to make sure to highlight those words, such as by using italic or bold font or all capital letters, to help make sure students see the essential word. As a general rule, you want to avoid negatively worded stems. Negatively worded stems include words like *none, never, not,* or *except,* such as "All of the following are correct except." Negative stems can be very tempting to write as they require you to come up with only one incorrect alternative response option. When a negatively worded stem tempts you, it may help to remember that asking students to identify an incorrect answer is not the same thing as asking them to identify a correct answer from among plausible alternatives. Another possible problem that can arise when using a negative stem is the double negative. That is, if your stem is negative, and any of your response options are negative, then you have created a confusing test item that becomes difficult to answer. In general, any item that requires more reasoning about the logic of the test item than it requires outcome-related knowledge is a poorly written item.

Most of the time multiple-choice items include a set of four possible alternatives, although this is not a hard-and-fast rule. You could decide to include any reasonable number of alternative response options, likely between three and six given what we know about the limits of our cognitive load capacity. When you write the alternative response options for a multiple-choice item, you want to include only plausibly correct options. Anytime you include a nonplausible response option, you reduce the difficulty of the item. For example, let's say your items include four alternatives each. This means students, if they were merely guessing, have a one-in-four chance of selecting the correct answer. If one of your alternatives is obviously nonplausible, such as listing a famous cartoon character as one of the four alternatives when asking students which theorist would have best predicted an example in the stem, then students will immediately eliminate the cartoon character as a choice and will have a one-in-three chance of selecting the correct answer on that item. Your nonplausible alternative means that students have a much better chance of guessing the correct answer, and your exam items are no longer consistent in their level of difficulty.

Other guidelines for writing alternative response options are really about making sure that you are testing achievement of the student learning outcome rather than your students' test-taking ability. These include making sure that your alternatives are grammatically consistent with the ending of your stem.

For example, if your stem ends in *a* or *an* then this a clue to which alternatives can be eliminated as options. Students know that if your stem ends in an incomplete sentence ending with the word *a* then the correct answer must begin with a consonant, and they should eliminate any alternatives beginning with vowels as plausible alternatives. The same kind of thing can happen when a stem ends in *is* or *are*. The obvious solution here is to end the stem in a way that captures multiple possibilities, such as *a/an* or *is/are*. Another guideline for writing alternatives is that they should be roughly consistent in length. Most students have been taught that alternatives for an item that are considerably longer or shorter than the others tend to be the correct choice, and in our experience this is usually right. Finally, we advise you to avoid "None of the above," "All of the above," or combined responses (e.g., "Both A and B are correct"), as these tend to test partial knowledge and reasoning ability. Typically, you do not have to know all of the information represented by the alternatives to get the correct answer when these types of response options are included.

True-False

For true-false items the student is to indicate whether a statement is true or false. When writing true-false items most of us are tempted to focus on small, factual details from material that was covered in one class or mentioned in a textbook. If these kinds of details are not critical to the student learning outcome you are assessing, then it is inappropriate to include them as test items for assessment.

Another thing to avoid when writing true-false test items is the negative statement. A negatively phrased true-false item is incredibly confusing as it requires the test taker to consider a double-negative situation. This is very difficult for students to try to reason through, which means you are not so much testing their knowledge of the outcome but are testing reasoning abilities. In addition, most of the time in this situation, it's possible to construct a convincing argument for a true answer and for a false answer, which means you will need to eliminate the item.

Absolute statements, like "always" or "never," should also be avoided in writing true-false statements. Students are generally aware that nothing is true all or none of the time, making these absolute statements a dead give-away as false. On the flip side, use qualifiers, like "usually" or "seldom," liberally. Many students have been taught that these types of qualifiers mean that a statement is true, and that will be such a student's default answer if he or she does not know the information being tested. By using qualifiers in both true and false statements you can reduce student students' ability to use these clues as ways to determine the correct answer and be better able to test their actual knowledge of concepts.

It is also important to avoid including more than one idea in a true-false item. As students are allowed to provide only one answer per item, then all of the ideas in the statement are either true or false. This means that students have to know only one of the ideas in order to answer the item correctly. If they know that one part is true, then the answer must be true, and vice versa. This means you are not testing knowledge of both pieces of the statement.

Finally, consider balancing the number of true and false statements and presenting them in a random way. This will reduce any potential benefit of guessing.

Matching

A matching item consists of two parallel lists of words or phrases that require students to match items on one list with items on the second list. It is very tempting when writing these to make one giant matching problem out of all of the things that you want to test students on, such as by listing all of the outcome-related terms in the first list and their definitions in the second list. This approach can create a potential cognitive overload for students by asking them to keep track of a great deal of information as they read through the lists. We have four tips that you can use to improve your matching items.

First, when you construct matching items you want to include no more than about seven items in each list. This will help prevent cognitive overload, as students should be able to keep track of what's in each list as they work through the problem. Second, make sure that the entire item fits onto one page. If the matching item splits over multiple pages, then students have to turn pages back and forth to see all of the listed items, which unnecessarily taxes the memory system and makes it difficult to answer the item. Remember, your goal is to test learning, not the cognitive load capacity of your students.

Third, make sure all components included in a particular matching item are related or come from the same subcategory of the knowledge being tested. You want to set up the problem so that students have to really understand the differences between the listed items in order to select the correct response. If the listed items come from different categories, then students only have to roughly know which items belong to which category in order to select the correct responses.

Finally, consider including an imperfect match between the number of items on one list and the possible number of responses on the other list. This will prevent students from using partial knowledge and the process of elimination to determine correct answers. If you use this approach, be sure to specify in your instructions that you can use responses more than once, and that some responses may not be used at all.

Best Practices for Constructed-Response Items

Constructed-response items require brief responses to specific questions or open-ended prompts and include such exam item types as short answer, labeling diagrams, and fill in the blank. These types of items can be used to assess just about any level of learning, from basic recall to the creation of new ideas. Constructed-response exam items will sometimes be designed so that they have a single-best answer, making them easy to score, but these exam items can also be designed so that you have to be open to accepting multiple possible responses as correct. Your exam key will need to reflect this openness. Let's look at a few brief guidelines for writing these types of exam items.

Short Answer

A short-answer item asks students a direct question that requires them to provide a brief answer, such as a word or a sentence or two, or even drawing an illustration. The key to short-answer items is to word the question so that the required answer is both brief and specific. In fact, it's a good idea if the exam instructions for short-answer items specify that you are looking for a brief answer. If the required answer is numerical, then you may want to instruct students as to the desired units to be used or the number of significant digits to be provided.

You can use a short-answer item to ask students to draw any object that was taught in the program that you expect them to be familiar with. You might combine the request to draw the object with a request to label parts of it or explain the functions of parts of it. Other things that you might ask students to illustrate include commonly understood ways of communicating information, like Venn diagrams, charts, graphs, and timelines.

Label a Diagram

The traditional label-a-diagram item includes presenting students with a diagram and asking them to label specific components. As long as your directions are clearly phrased, the request to label can be made in a number of ways. You can ask students to simply label a set number of parts (e.g., indicate the name and location of any five components within the diagram), provide the labels for indicated parts (e.g., provide the name of each of the indicated components shown in the diagram), or indicate where components are located in the diagram (e.g., indicate the location of the listed components). Two key things for successful label-a-diagram types of questions are that the diagram is a simple, clear, neat illustration and that there is enough room to place labels in the appropriate locations.

Fill in the Blank

Fill-in-the-blank items involve presenting students with an incomplete sentence and asking them to fill in the missing word, number, or symbol. The temptation with these is to take sentences directly from the textbook or a lecture slide and remove a couple of words. While this is easy, it is better if you reword statements so that the exam item is a new presentation of the information. This will allow you to test student understanding of the idea, rather than their ability to recall a familiar sentence.

You should word the incomplete statements in such a way that the missing information to be filled in is both brief and specific. It is a good idea to include only one or two blank spaces in a single statement, so that students understand what is being asked and do not feel like they are trying to piece together a puzzle. The blank spaces for each answer should be equal in length, so that the length of a blank space is not seen as a clue to the length of the required answer. If students are to write their answers in those blank spaces, make sure there is sufficient room to respond. Finally, as with multiple-choice stems, you'll want to be aware of how your grammar may influence responses. Be aware that if the word *a* or *an* or *is* or *are* precedes a blank space, then this is a cue to students in search of the right answer.

Best Practices for Essay Items

Essay items ask students to respond to a prompt and allow that response to be determined by the student. Essay items are used for assessing deeper levels of learning, like the ability to integrate ideas, justify a decision, or critique a design. A good essay item clearly asks students to respond to a specific question or prompt.

Essay items have the benefit of allowing students to demonstrate complex learning, which takes quite a bit of time for students to do. This means that you are limited to asking a small number of essay questions in any one exam. Scoring essay items requires the use of a rubric. For guidelines on how to create and apply a rubric, check out module 7, "Rubrics: Creating and Using Rubrics for Program Assessment."

Summary

A well-designed exam will provide actionable information about student achievement of your program learning outcomes; results will tell you exactly what it is that students have learned and what they didn't so that you know what to target for improvement. Including multiple program faculty in the process of writing your exam will help to make sure that multiple perspectives are included and reduce the amount of time it takes to develop a complete exam. To help keep the entire exam process manageable, we encourage you to use Microsoft Excel to analyze your exam item data. You'll find instructions for how to analyze your exam data (including rubric data from essay items) in module 10, "Organizing, Summarizing, and Presenting Your Evidence: Using Microsoft Excel to Make Sense of Your Data."

9

SURVEYS

Finding Out What Your Students Think

When you want to know what students believe they have learned, understand the kinds of learning behaviors they have engaged in, or their thoughts about how your program's curriculum has contributed to their learning, then a survey is most likely the assessment measurement tool you want to use. Surveys are considered an indirect form of assessment, as they do not show you what students have learned, but rather provide student opinions about their learning and experiences (for a more detailed explanation of direct and indirect measures, see module 6, "Assessment Measurement Tools: Determining What Your Students Are Learning"). Typically, you'll want to use a survey as a supplement to a more direct measure of learning, such as that produced from exams (see module 8, "Exams: Asking Questions That Provide the Answers You Need") or from applying rubrics to student work (see module 7, "Rubrics: Creating and Using Rubrics for Program Assessment"). A major benefit of using surveys is that you can design one survey to gather information about all of your student learning outcomes.

Responses to a survey are especially useful for providing insights into the evidence of learning produced by your direct measures. For example, let's say your rubric data show you that students are not meeting your expectations for most components of your written communication outcome. In responding to your survey, students indicated that they believe they have very strong writing skills and that they almost never write more than a single draft of a paper before they submit it. In this example, the survey results shed quite a bit of light on the rubric results. It appears that your students are very confident in their writing abilities and, perhaps as a consequence of this, have stopped engaging in the important step of revising their writing before considering it finished. This combination of information points to some very specific actions that faculty in your program can take to improve writing, such as stressing the importance of the revision process, requiring first drafts to be submitted, and sharing the written communication rubric with students to help clarify expectations for successful writing.

In this module, we share a four-step process for creating a survey that will help you to better understand student learning in your program. We also discuss considerations for deciding how to administer your survey and provide an introduction to coding open-ended responses. Coding is a process that allows you to see patterns in those open-ended responses, which helps you reach conclusions about what students have shared.

Creating a Survey

The process of creating a survey requires four steps. As with other assessment activities, it is best to complete these steps with a partner or small committee. The inclusion of multiple perspectives in the process will help you to create a survey that provides a richer picture of the student experience. In addition, working with others allows you to split up the workload, which helps to keep it manageable for everyone involved. The four steps to create your survey are:

1. Determine what you wish to know.
2. Write your questions.
3. Configure your survey.
4. Review and finalize your survey.

Let's look at what's involved in each of these steps.

Step 1: Determine What You Wish to Know

Before you start writing survey questions, you must decide what it is you want to learn from your survey. By determining what you wish to know from your students, you'll make sure to ask questions that will get you the desired information. In addition, you'll avoid asking questions that will not help you with your assessment process. By keeping your survey focused on what you need to know and not asking extraneous questions, you will avoid wasting your students' time in responding and not leave yourself wondering what to do with the information those extra questions gave you.

A survey that is designed for assessment purposes needs to focus primarily on understanding student learning outcome achievement. This means that your first step will be to identify the outcome (or outcomes) your survey will ask about. For each outcome, you then want to decide what it is you want to know about your students' experience of that outcome. Typically, you'll want to know about your students' perceived level of accomplishment of the outcome, but beyond this basic information the possibilities are endless.

In deciding what you want to know, it can help to think about how you will ultimately use the information you gather. In other words, the things you learn should be actionable. For example, if you are designing a survey as part of your assessment of your oral communication student learning outcome, then actionable things you might want to learn about include the number of oral presentation assignments students complete in your program, the number of courses in your program that include instruction in how to give oral presentations, and the kinds of activities students engage in when preparing to give an oral presentation. However, you would not necessarily want to ask students if they believe that oral presentation skills are important to develop. Understanding the student experience of oral presentation assignments and instruction can help you better understand your curriculum and make changes as needed, but knowing how students feel about the importance of the outcome is not necessarily something you can take action to improve (although anything is possible!).

To complete this first step, you'll want to brainstorm a list of all the possible outcome-related experiences, behaviors, and attitudes that you wish to know about. You'll then want to review your list to make sure that the items on it will provide you with usable (i.e., actionable) information. Including multiple faculty in this process will help you to make sure that you are capturing necessary information and that there is agreement on its potential to help you take informed actions for improving your program.

Step 2: Write Your Questions

The items on the list you generated in Step 1 will serve as the basis of your survey questions. To write your questions, you'll need to determine what types of questions you wish to ask (e.g., rating scales, open-ended), and then write effective questions. Let's look at the three most popular types of survey questions and then go over some general tips for writing clear and effective questions.

Response-Scale Survey Items

Response-scale items are probably the most commonly used survey item type, as they are easy for respondents to answer and can be used to ask about alomst any self-perception, attitude, or behavior. Technically, response-scale items are not questions. A response-scale item presents a statement and asks the respondent to indicate their response to the statement using a scale. You might expect to see a scale item like the following on an assessment survey focusing on an oral communication learning outcome:

Please indicate how much you agree with the following statement:
I am capable of giving oral presentations that address the needs of my audience.

1	2	3	4	5
Strongly Disagree	*Disagree*	*Neither Agree nor Disagree*	*Agree*	*Strongly Agree*

A survey on oral communication skills might have several such scale items, one for each skill that is considered a component of the oral communication outcome.

   While the agree scale shown in the previous example is a commonly used scale for these types of survey items, you can use scales to ask students to indicate how often a behavior is engaged in (i.e., never, sometimes, about half of the time, most of the time, always), or rate their abilities (i.e., poor, fair, good, very good, excellent), the impact of the program (i.e., not at all, a little, somewhat, a fair amount, a great deal), and more. The key with rating scales is to label every point on the scale so that its meaning is clear and understood in the same way by everyone. In addition, it is considered good practice to use the same response scale for all of the response-scale items within your survey. This way your respondents will not be confused by changing scales and will generally have an easier time filling out your survey. If you do need to include multiple types of scales in your survey, then you will want to group your survey items by scale type in order to reduce confusion.

   Once you have chosen a scale, you will want to be sure to arrange it in a logical order, typically with the most negative or lowest option on the left and the most positive or highest option on the right. The numerical values of your scale should be set so that the lowest option on the scale is assigned a 1, with the numbers ascending along with the options. This way higher scores on the scale indicate more of the ability or a more positive attitude. Response scales usually have either five or seven options to choose from. The odd number of options on a response scale allows for a middle value, which can be a neutral response as it is in the previous example. Neutral middle values allow the respondent to express a lack of opinion or strong feeling one way or the other on a particular item.

Multiple-Choice Survey Questions

Multiple-choice survey items ask a question and then provide a set of possible response options. The items can be designed so that the respondent is asked to provide only one answer or to indicate all of the answers that apply. Multiple-choice survey questions are especially good for asking for factual information. For example, on an oral communication assessment survey, you might ask students about the campus resources they took advantage of to improve their abilities:

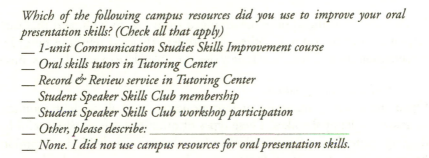

Which of the following campus resources did you use to improve your oral presentation skills? (Check all that apply)
___ *1-unit Communication Studies Skills Improvement course*
___ *Oral skills tutors in Tutoring Center*
___ *Record & Review service in Tutoring Center*
___ *Student Speaker Skills Club membership*
___ *Student Speaker Skills Club workshop participation*
___ *Other, please describe: _____*
___ *None. I did not use campus resources for oral presentation skills.*

One thing to note about this example is that the option presented after the list of known resources is an open-ended invitation to list additional resources (i.e., "Other, please describe:___"). This invitation can be particularly useful if you are not absolutely certain that you've captured all of the possible response options. The "other" response is placed at the end of the list of known resources so that your students have a chance to review all of the listed options before deciding that their response has not already been provided to them as a choice. A "none" option is included after this as a last possible response so that a student who has not used campus resources may still answer the question. Otherwise, if a student did not provide an answer, it would be impossible for you to know if this was because the student did not use campus resources or because he or she skipped the question.

An additional note about this example is that the response options are presented in alphabetical order, with the exception of the "other" and "none" options, which should always appear last in a set of possible responses. As much as it is possible, the response options for a multiple-choice item should be presented in a logical order, such as alphabetically or from low to high. This will make it easy for your students to find the correct responses and reduce the possibility that they miss relevant options.

A final thing to consider in writing your response options for a multiple-choice survey question is that when you have numerical response options those options need to be mutually exclusive. For example, if you want to know how often students rehearse their presentations, then you might ask them the following:

On average, how many times do you rehearse a presentation before you give it in class?
___ *0 times*
___ *1–3 times*
___ *4–6 times*
___ *7 or more times*

You'll notice that the options are arranged from low to high, and that each response is distinct from the others. If a student typically rehearses his or her presentation three times, there is only one possible place to give that response.

Open-Ended Survey Questions

Open-ended survey questions present a question and allow the respondent to answer as he or she likes. These types of questions can be very useful for digging deeper into a topic, understanding the rationale behind an opinion, or even asking students to demonstrate their knowledge, much like a test question. For example, on your oral communication assessment survey you might ask senior students to help you understand what experiences were the most useful to them, such as:

> *During the last four years, which experience(s) has been most helpful in preparing you to give good oral presentations?*

This type of question has a benefit of allowing you to know exactly what your students think. That said, there is a risk with asking an open-ended question that your respondents will not provide useful or relevant information. In addition, many people do not enjoy responding to open-ended survey questions and will skip them if possible. This means that there is a risk that only a few students will actually answer the open-ended items.

Another thing to consider when including open-ended questions in your survey is that it takes a few extra steps to extract useful, meaningful information from the responses. The process of extracting that information is called "coding," and we provide a basic introduction to this process later in this module. Coding helps you to make sure that you consider all of the available information in your students' responses. Otherwise the temptation is to just read through what students wrote and pick out the interesting bits. This pick-and-choose approach can be very misleading. As humans, we tend to pay attention to the one or two negative answers or the one or two really stellar answers and let those few examples sway how we see the entire set of responses. This rather informal approach can mean that you miss useful, actionable information and instead expend resources on things that are not needed.

In general, because of the drawbacks, it is a good idea to use open-ended survey questions sparingly. Think of them as special tools that you pull out only when nothing else will quite do.

Tips for Writing Clear, Effective Survey Questions
If you've ever tried to answer a poorly worded question, then you know how important it is to write clearly phrased survey questions. A poorly phrased survey question can result in either respondents skipping the question or meaningless answers that you will have difficulty interpreting and acting on. Fortunately, we have a few guidelines that you can follow to improve the clarity and quality of your questions.

First, it is important to remember that survey respondents do not typically want to put a lot of time or effort into understanding your questions. This means that you should use language that is clear, simple, and to the point. As much as possible, avoid the use of jargon or complex words or terms. Even though you know your students should know what these things mean, a survey question is not the place to test that knowledge and risk their not understanding what you are asking. Do not include unnecessary details or text in your survey questions. Generally, you want to try to find a way to ask your questions in as straightforward a manner as possible.

Second, ask only one thing in each question. Asking more than one thing within a single question is known as asking a double-barreled question. For example, this double-barreled item could mistakenly have been included in your oral communication assessment survey:

> *How often did your oral presentation assignments require the use of a visual aid and the submission of a written document in support of your presentation?*
> ___ *Never*
> ___ *Sometimes*
> ___ *About half of the time*
> ___ *Most of the time*
> ___ *Every single time*

The visual aid requirement and the written document requirement are two separate things. If students were always required to use a visual aid and had to submit a written document only some of the time, they would not be able to provide a single answer to this question. Even if you allowed them to select more than one answer, you'd have a difficult time knowing which answer went to which component of the question. Even in the case of open-ended questions, double-barrels can create a situation where the respondent answers only part of the question, leaving you with less information than you desired.

You can almost always recognize a double-barreled question by the use of the word *and* within it. If, after you have drafted questions, you find you've written one that includes the word *and,* you will want to seriously consider splitting that question into two questions, or as many as needed to remove the use of *and* in the question. Our previous double-barreled example could easily be asked as two questions, thus removing any possible confusion.

A third key thing to avoid in writing your closed-ended survey questions is the creation of a double-negative situation. If your question has a negative in it (e.g., none, did not, never), and your response options also include negatives (e.g., never, no, disagree), then you've created a situation where a negative response actually means something positive. For example, consider how you would respond to this item:

Please indicate how much you agree with the following statement:
I did not use the Record & Review service as often as I needed it.

1	2	3	4	5
Strongly Disagree	*Disagree*	*Neither Agree nor Disagree*	*Agree*	*Strongly Agree*

In this case, if you feel that you did use the service as often as it was needed, then the correct response is either "Strongly Disagree" or "Disagree." Answering double-negative questions like this feels a bit like solving a logic problem. You may have students provide the incorrect answer because they did not follow the logic correctly, or you may have students choose not to answer the question because it confused them. You can easily resolve double-negative situations like this by converting the statement into a positive one, such as, "I used the Record & Review service as often as I needed it."

Step 3: Configure Your Survey

After you've written your questions, your next step is to set up the survey in a respondent-friendly, logical manner. Your survey questions should be framed by an introduction at the start and a thank-you at the end. These opening and closing notes should indicate the general purpose of the survey, including some explanation of how the results will be used, how long the survey will take (if you know this), whom to contact should the respondent have questions, and whether the results will be either confidential or anonymous. An anonymous survey is one in which you cannot connect responses to the individual who provided them. A confidential survey means that you do know who provided each response, but you will not reveal that information. For example, the introduction to the oral communication survey might read:

Welcome to the oral communication skills assessment survey. This survey is intended to help your faculty understand student achievement of the oral communication learning outcome. We will use this information to make improvements to our program, such as by changing the ways we teach oral communication skills or the courses that we offer. The survey should take between 10 and 15 minutes to complete. Your responses will be kept confidential. If you have any questions about the survey, or how we will use the results, please contact me at prof123@state-u.edu. I thank you in advance for sharing your thoughts with us in this survey.

The thank-you at the end of the survey would contain much of the same information but begin with a note of thanks.

Between the introduction and the closing thank-you, you will want to ask your questions in a logical order. Generally, it is a good idea to start with easy or interesting questions in order to ease your student respondents into the survey. For example, if you've told students that this survey is about assessment of learning outcomes, then it makes sense to open the survey by asking students to self-rate their achievement of said learning outcomes. They will find these questions fairly easy to answer, and the questions will make sense given what they know about the topic of the survey, which will likely entice them to continue to fill out the survey. Your questions should be grouped by topic so that your students can focus their memory and attention on one topic at a time, making the survey easier to respond to accurately. If you are using multiple item types, then you will also want to consider grouping items within each topic by item type.

If you need to ask demographic questions like student age, sex, or employment experiences, then these questions should go at the end. In addition, you might consider including a "Decline to state" option on these types of questions, allowing students the freedom to choose to answer or not. *Demographic questions* are, by definition, personal in nature. Allowing the freedom to decline to answer tends to make respondents feel more comfortable about providing such personal information. In addition, after answering all of your content questions, respondents tend to feel invested in the survey and more willing to provide personal details.

Step 4: Review and Finalize Your Survey

Before you invite your students to fill out your survey, it is a very good idea to ask a few people to take it and share their feedback on the questions, their experience in filling it out, and even how long it took them to complete the survey. You can ask faculty to do this test for you, or even ask students. If you have student workers in your program, then you might ask them to complete the survey during their time working in the program, using the opportunity to teach them a bit about assessment and survey design. Finally, some institutions offer professional survey review services through the assessment or institutional research office, and we encourage you to reach out to check if this is available at your institution.

Use what you learn from your trial run to edit your survey. If you made any significant changes to the survey, you might ask a colleague or student or two to review those changes to make sure that things are now clear. The last step before you consider your survey ready is to give the survey one final proofread. You want to make sure that the survey is free of typos or other errors that might create confusion in your survey respondents.

The Institutional Review Board

An important thing to consider before you administer your survey is whether or not it needs to go before your institution's Institutional Review Board (IRB). The IRB examines plans for research that involves human participants. Their job is to ensure that the rights and welfare of participants in that research are protected. Generally, if your survey for assessment purposes focuses on learning and learning-related behaviors and will be used only internally (e.g., you won't share the results at a conference or in a publication), then your survey will be exempt from IRB review. If you plan to share your survey results externally (even informally, such as through discussion), then before you administer your survey you need to contact your IRB and apply for review. If you are including questions in your survey that focus on topics not related to assessment or basic quality assurance (e.g., satisfaction with your program) then you might need to go through the IRB, and we encourage you to reach out and ask them before you send your survey to students. As a rule, it is always better to be safe and check with the IRB before you send out your survey than it is to potentially run into a research ethics problem after you've started.

Administering Your Survey

There are two basic approaches to administering your survey: on paper or online. The two approaches somewhat counterbalance each other in terms of benefits and drawbacks that must be considered in deciding which approach to use. When administered on paper, the survey is usually given to students during a class meeting or other in-person session. You can watch the students fill it out, and with rare exception, all of them will fill out the survey. Getting a 100% response rate is a major benefit of using this approach. The drawback is that you then have to enter all of the responses into Microsoft Excel or your other data analysis software. This process is time-consuming and includes the risk of making data entry errors.

If you administer the survey online, however, then the data will be available to download into your data analysis software, saving you a lot of data entry time and error risk. Some online survey tools take this a step further and provide data analysis tools, so that with a few clicks you can generate graphs or basic statistics to help you understand your survey responses. The downside of administering your survey online is that it is very difficult to get all of your students to fill it out. On most college and university campuses, students receive many requests to fill out surveys each semester. Your request may get lost in the shuffle or ignored because students are simply tired both of being asked to fill out surveys and actually filling out surveys.

If you decide to go with an online survey administration, there are ways to increase your response rate. First, talk to students about the survey. Let them know it is coming and that their participation is important to you. Receiving an in-person request from someone that they know, and presumably care about, will increase the likelihood that they fill out your survey. Second, consider giving them time in class to fill out the online survey. Most students have a smartphone, tablet, or laptop that they can be invited to bring to class and use to fill out the survey. Third, consider offering an incentive for filling out the survey. Incentives do not have to be expensive to work, and not everyone has to receive an incentive. In fact, holding a drawing for something unique that students cannot get elsewhere can be very motivating. We've worked with programs that have great success offering books written and signed by a program faculty member, a homemade dinner at a faculty member's home, or lunch with a special guest speaker who is slated to come to the campus soon.

Considering Other Surveys at Your Institution

Some institutions conduct regular online surveys of all students or of specific groups of students, such as graduating seniors. If your institutions does conduct such surveys, then you will want to consider a couple of things before you administer your survey. First, it may be possible to add a few items to an existing survey. Many institutions allow programs to do this in order to reduce the overall number of survey requests that students receive. In such a situation, the institution-wide survey would be designed so that only students in your program will see your program's questions. Second, if it is not possible to collaborate, then you will want to consider the timing of the institution-wide survey in determining when to administer your program's survey. You want to allow some time (at a minimum a few days) between the requests to complete the institution's survey and your program's survey. This way your students do not feel overwhelmed by survey requests and will be more likely to respond to both surveys.

Making Sense of Student Responses

After you've administered your survey, you need to figure out what the responses tell you. For closed-ended items, including response-scale items and multiple-choice items, we recommend that you use Microsoft Excel to analyze your responses. An explanation of how to do this is provided in module 10, "Organizing, Summarizing, and Presenting Your Evidence: Using Microsoft Excel to Make Sense of Your Data."

For open-ended survey items, you will need to code what students wrote. Coding is the process of identifying themes or categories within the open-ended survey responses. This process will help you distinguish meaningful patterns in the responses that would be difficult to see if you read only your students' responses. There are two basic approaches to determining the codes in your responses. One is to approach the responses with a set of predetermined codes in mind. In this approach, you are looking for responses that align with your expected codes. To use this approach for each student response, you tally how often each of your predetermined codes occurred.

The other approach is to let the codes emerge from the responses. Here you assign codes to each meaningful segment of text as you encounter it, keeping track of the codes you assign so that you can apply them to each response that speaks to the same theme. This approach to coding involves two steps. The first step is to freely generate codes as you go through the responses. You do this first step without concern for the number of codes you come up with, or whether the codes overlap in content. Once you've done this for all of your responses, you then go back and review your codes. The second step is to combine small, related categories into a larger code; eliminate redundant codes; and if you have a code that has a very high number of responses assigned to it, then you might consider reviewing those responses to determine if you need to break the code up into more than one code.

Whichever way you approach coding, it is important that you keep the codes you assign connected to the student responses that led to those codes. This will allow you to go back and read exactly what each response that was assigned a code said, which can help both in the process of refining your codes and in the process of making decisions for improvement. The way that we like to approach coding is to create a Microsoft Excel spreadsheet that has student responses in the first column, one response per row, and the codes across subsequent columns, one code per column. This approach will allow you to create as many codes as you like and keep them all in one place. By using the number 1 to indicate when a code has occurred in a particular response, you can then sort the responses by a particular code, and even ask Excel to sum how many times each code has occurred. Instructions for how to set up an Excel spreadsheet and sum columns of data are provided in module 10, "Organizing, Summarizing, and Presenting Your Evidence: Using Microsoft Excel to Make Sense of Your Data."

Ultimately, regardless of which coding approach you choose, your goal is to be able to describe the themes that have appeared in your responses and how often each of those themes appeared. This will help you distinguish whether something was important to one or two students or whether it was a theme that appeared in the majority of your students' responses, or somewhere in between these two extremes. This ability to enumerate the responses will help you to make well-informed decisions about student learning.

Summary

Survey responses can provide insight into your students' experiences, behaviors, and perceptions of their learning. When this indirect evidence of learning is considered alongside more direct measures of learning, such as information from exam items or rubrics applied to student work, a rich picture of student learning develops. The key is to design your survey so that it will provide information on which you are able to act. By following the four-step process to create a survey and making well-considered decisions about how and when to administer your survey, you will be well on your way to actionable evidence.

ORGANIZING, SUMMARIZING, AND PRESENTING YOUR EVIDENCE

Using Microsoft Excel to Make Sense of Your Data

A key component of meaningful assessment is the use of evidence to guide decision-making. Making sense of your evidence typically involves analyzing quantitative data. If you are like the majority of the faculty with whom we work, just the word *data* can make assessment seem intimidating. Fortunately, once you've generated scores from your evidence, such as rubric, exam item, or survey response scores, the process of turning those scores into easy-to-understand data is simple to do with Microsoft Excel.

Microsoft Excel is an incredibly powerful tool for understanding all kinds of data. As such, it has a number of menus and lots of possible options within each of those menus, the majority of which you will not need in order to organize, summarize, or present your assessment data. We want to point you toward the features that you will use as part of your assessment process so that hopefully you will not be overwhelmed by all of the possibilities. In this module we present an introduction to setting up your Excel spreadsheet, explain how to perform the most commonly used analyses to summarize assessment data, and show you how to create the tables and charts that will help you to present your findings to your colleagues. Finally, we provide some specific tips on how to work with data that come from rubrics, exams, and surveys.

The best way to read this module is to open Excel on your computer and follow along. We'll give you example data and walk you through the steps of entering it into Excel, summarizing and describing that data and presenting it in easy-to-read tables and charts. We also create a few brief videos that walk you through the steps we describe and include a few additional tools, tips, and tricks. To view the videos visit https://sty.presswarehouse.com/Books/BookDetail.aspx?productID=484608

Organizing Your Assessment Data

Excel's Layout

One of the things that we happen to love about Microsoft Excel is that it provides a clear, consistent structure for organizing your data. Regardless of what types of data you have, or what you want to learn from them, the setup of an Excel spreadsheet remains the same. So, let's get familiar with that setup. If you are following along, you'll notice that when you open Excel it presents you with a number of templates, or options, for getting started. Select a blank workbook. A blank workbook is a spreadsheet; it looks like a grid or a table with rows and columns that fill most of the screen.

The first thing we want you to note is that columns are labeled with letters, starting with *A* and going all the way through the alphabet. If you go beyond *Z* you'll see that the alphabet repeats beginning with *AA*, so *AA, AB, AC* and so on. The number of columns you can include in your spreadsheet is virtually limitless, so you never have to worry about having too many. The second thing we want you to notice is that the rows are labeled with numbers, beginning with 1. Again the maximum number of possible rows you can create is so great that you will likely never run out of possible rows to use.

The cells in the spreadsheet are labeled by their placement at the intersection of a column and row. When you place your cursor in any cell in the table, you'll see the label for that cell appear in the upper left-hand corner at the top of the spreadsheet. If you click in the very first cell, the one in the first column, A, and the first row, 1, you are in Cell A1. You should see the label A1 in the box in the left-hand corner of the spreadsheet. The cells of your Excel spreadsheet are where you will type the labels for the rows and columns, as well as the scores or responses that you have collected.

Organizing Your Spreadsheet

The order that you enter your evidence into a spreadsheet follows a basic set of rules. The first of these rules is that rows represent people. This means that each student will be assigned a single row. The second rule is that columns represent data points. This means that each thing you have a score for, such as each rubric component, exam item, or survey response, gets its own column. In Excel, you type the labels for each column in the first row, with the first column labeled so that it's clear it will contain the names of your students; if you have assigned codes to your students, then those codes will go in the first column.

For those of you following along in Excel, we want you to work with an example set of data that came from applying the written communication rubric presented in Figure 7.1 to a set of student papers. To organize your Excel spreadsheet, we want you to type "Student" in Cell A1 as the label for column A. Columns B through F should be labeled with the components of the written communication rubric, which are Style, Mechanics, Thesis Statement, Organization, and Supporting Evidence. Once your spreadsheet has an organized setup, it's time to enter your students' names and scores.

Entering Your Scores

The way you go about entering your scores into the spreadsheet's cells is up to you. There are two primary ways to approach the task: enter the scores by student, filling out the spreadsheet row by row, or enter the scores by data point, filling out the spreadsheet column by column. The key to entering your scores quickly, and to reducing the risk of making an error in your entry, is to pick one approach and use it consistently. Regardless of how you approach the data-entry process, you will want to review your data entry to check for any entry errors or empty cells before you proceed to analyze your data. It is possible to have empty cells in a spreadsheet—for example, when a student does not answer a survey question, you will not have a value to enter into that cell—but for most types of assessment data empty cells are rare. When you do enter your data into Excel, be sure to save it often to avoid accidentally losing your work.

If you are following along in Excel, the next step is to enter the example data that are shown in Table 10.1.

Summarizing Your Assessment Data

The ability to easily analyze data is one of the primary reasons for using Excel. Because of this, Excel has created many different ways to access the formulas you need to run analyses. For example, there is a Formulas tab that contains many options. Alternatively, as all formulas begin with an equals sign (i.e., =) if you type an equals sign into any cell, then Excel assumes you want to write a formula and both produces a drop-down menu of commonly used formulas and starts a formula bar just above your data for you to type in that formula.

For assessment purposes, you will need to know and use only a very small number of formulas, which are easy to access from the Auto Sum feature that

TABLE 10.1
Example Written Communication Rubric Scores for 10 Students

Student	Style	Mechanics	Thesis Statement	Organization	Supporting Evidence
Dana	4	3	1	3	3
Taylor	1	2	1	1	1
Casey	1	2	1	2	2
Jamie	3	3	2	3	3
Morgan	3	3	2	3	3
Pat	3	4	2	4	3
Sam	2	2	1	2	2
Charlie	3	4	2	3	3
Dakota	4	4	3	4	4
Andy	4	4	4	4	4

Note. If you are following along in Excel, enter the scores for these students in your spreadsheet.

is available on the Home tab. The Auto Sum feature is located toward the upper right-hand corner of the Home tab in the Editing section. In addition to the words *Auto Sum*, you'll see a capital sigma (i.e., Σ) next to it. The formulas most commonly used for assessment include sum, average, standard deviation, and frequencies. Let's go over how to compute these, as well as how to write your own formula in order to calculate a percentage.

A good rule of thumb to follow before computing any analysis is to make sure there is a clear label for that analysis. Labels are most often typed in the cell just next to the one where you insert your analysis.

Sum

The Sum formula adds up all of the cells that you have selected to be summed. To ask Excel to sum values for you, place your cursor in the empty cell just below the column of data you wish to sum up. Next, select the Sum formula from the Auto Sum drop-down menu. This will insert the formula into the cell you selected and highlight the cells above it in your column. Be sure to label what will be in this cell, such as by placing the word *sum* in the empty cell next to it.

By default Excel will select only the numerical values in the column above your formula, which means it knows not to include your column label in Row 1 (e.g., Cell B1). If, however, you wanted to sum up a subset of cells, such as B2 through B5, then you can either type the first and last cell numbers into the formula that appears or use your mouse to select the cells you want to add up before you hit Enter to run the computation.

If you are following along in Excel, let's compute the sum for each of the rubric components. To start, type the label "Sum" in Cell A12, which should be just below your student names. Click Cell B12, then click the Auto Sum drop-down menu, and select Sum from the list. You should see the formula "=SUM(B2:B11)" appear. This means that when you hit Enter, the sum of Cells B2 through B11 will appear in the designated cell. Repeat the process of computing the sum for each of the components.

Average

The Average formula computes the mathematical average for the cells you have selected. To ask Excel to compute the average, place your cursor in an empty cell just below the column of data you wish to average. Next, select the Average formula from the drop-down menu. This will insert the formula into the cell you selected and highlight the numerical cells above it in your column. Hit Enter to compute the average. Be sure to provide a label next to this cell so that you remember what the numbers in it represent.

If you are following along in Excel, let's compute the average for each of our rubric components. Begin by typing the label "Average" in Cell A13. Then click into Cell B13 to insert the Average formula. The Average formula automatically includes all the numerical cells above it, in this case, Cells B2 through B12, which means that the sum you computed in Cell B12 would be included in the computation of the average. Since the sum is not one of the numbers in our data set and should not be included in the computation of our average, we need to tell Excel to average only the scores in Cells B2 through B11. To do this, you can either type in the correct cell labels or use your mouse to highlight the cells you wish to average. Once you have told Excel which cells to average, hit the Enter key to show the calculated average. Repeat this process for each of the rubric components.

Standard Deviation

The standard deviation tells you how spread out in relation to the average the values in your set of data are. Stats people typically report standard deviation alongside the average as it helps to paint a picture of the distribution of scores in the set. For example, if you have an average score of 2.5 on a 4-point rubric, and a standard deviation of 0.5, it means that the majority of your students fall between a 2 and a 3 on that rubric and are relatively tightly grouped together. If, however, the standard deviation is 1.5, then your students are more widely spread out between a 1 and a 4. Knowing the standard deviation helps to enrich the description of your data that was provided by the average.

If you and your program colleagues are not stats people, and you are not certain everyone will understand what the standard deviation is telling you, please feel free to skip it. You want to present information that is useful to your colleagues for making decisions, not confuse them with information that is not clearly understood. Besides, you can essentially replace the standard deviation and still understand the spread of your scores by looking at a table showing the number of times each score occurred or a stacked bar chart presenting this information.

To ask Excel to compute the standard deviation of a set of scores, start by placing your cursor in an empty cell, such as the one just below the average you computed for a column of data. Then go to your Auto Sum drop-down menu and select More Functions. In the Search for a Function box that appears, type "Standard Deviation" and then click Go. This will produce a list of possible functions for you to select from. You want to select STDEV, and hit OK. Next a Function Arguments box appears. Click in the Number 1 box, then highlight the cells containing the data you want to compute standard deviation for, and click OK to calculate it.

For those of you following along, let's type the label "SD" (for "standard deviation") in Cell A14. Click in Cell B14 and follow the steps to compute standard deviation for Cells B2 through B11. Repeat this process for each of the rubric components.

Frequency

A frequency is simply a count of all the times a specified score occurred. Knowing the frequency of each possible score on a rubric component, an exam item, or a survey item will help you understand the distribution of your scores. For example, let's say your average score on a 4-point rubric component is 3. This might lead you to believe that your students are generally demonstrating that rubric component satisfactorily. Yet if you were to look at your frequencies, you might see that half of your students are earning a 4 on the rubric, doing better than the goal of earning a 3, and half of your students are earning a 2 on the rubric, falling below your goal of 3. Knowing the frequency distribution of your scores would help you to make better decisions about student learning than just knowing the average alone.

As you will want to compute frequencies for each possible score in your data set, it makes the most sense to first set up a place to put all of those frequencies. A table setup works well for this task. Start your table in a cell that is separate from your entered data. You'll want to make a column for each data point (e.g., rubric component), and in this case you want a row for each

TABLE 10.2
Layout for a Frequencies Table for the Written Communication Rubric Data Shared in Table 10.1

Frequencies	Style	Mechanics	Thesis Statement	Organization	Supporting Evidence
Novice (1)					
Developing (2)					
Proficient (3)					
Accomplished (4)					

possible score (e.g., performance levels), as well as a label to indicate what will be in this table.

For those of you following along, start your frequencies table by typing the label "Frequencies" in Cell H1. In Cells I1 through M1, type the labels for your rubric components (or copy and paste them from Cells B1 through F1). In Cells H2 through H5 type your levels of performance. The empty table will look like that shown in Table 10.2.

Once set up, you'll want to fill in the cells of your table by asking Excel to compute how often each specific score occurred. To do this you will use the COUNTIF function. To get this function, place your cursor in the first cell of your table. In our example this is the cell for the Novice (1) level of the Style component (Cell I2 for those of you following along). Next, go to your Formulas drop-down menu and select More Functions. In the Search for a Function box that appears, type "COUNTIF" and then click Go. This will produce a list of possible functions for you to select from, and COUNTIF should be at the top of the list. Select it to see the Function Arguments box appear. This box asks you for two things. The first is the Range. The range is the set of scores you want Excel to examine. Since we are looking at the Style component, we need to use our mouse to select all of the scores in the Style column (Cells B2 through B11 in our example). The second thing that we need to tell Excel is the Criteria to count. As we are in the Novice (1) row of our frequencies table, we want to tell Excel to use the criterion of 1, so type a "1" into the Criteria box and then click OK. Excel will then insert the total number of 1s earned by students on the Style component into the designated cell. Repeat this process for each score on each rubric component to fill in your table.

Before we leave the COUNTIF function, we want to point out that you can use it to count any designated criterion. So, for example, if you have multiple-choice answers in your spreadsheet, you could count how often an A, a B, a C, or a D was given as an answer.

Percentages

Percentages and frequencies tell us the same basic information about the distribution of scores in our data; however, percentages can be easier to understand as they use a standard metric. For example, most of us have an easy time understanding what it means when we say that 20% of our students got an exam item correct, whereas it can be more difficult to understand what it means when we say 14 students out of 70 got the item correct. For this reason, you might want to convert your frequencies table into a table of percentages.

To do this, you'll first need a blank table set up with the same column and row labels as you used for your frequencies table, although this time you want to label your table "Percentages." For ease in calculating your percentages we recommend that you place this new table just below your frequencies table. To compute percentages, you will have to type in a simple formula. To get started, place your cursor in the first cell of the table, then type an equals sign (i.e., =) in the cell to tell Excel you want to compute something. Next click on the corresponding cell in the frequencies table. Then type a forward slash (i.e., /) to tell Excel you want to divide this number by something. Finally, type the total number of scores in your data set. Hit Enter to get the percentage of students in that cell of your table.

If you are following along, create a table starting with the label Percentages in Cell H7. In Cell I8 type an equals sign, then click on Cell I2, and then type forward slash 10, which will appear as =I2/10. Hit Enter to see the percentage in decimal form. Repeat this process for each of the cells in your percentages table. Once this is done, highlight the cells in your percentages table and then click on the percent sign (i.e., %) near the center of the Home tab ribbon above. This will convert your decimal figures into more familiar percentage figures.

Presenting Your Assessment Data

When it comes to presenting your data, you want to do it in a way that will make sense to your program colleagues. If you are the kind of people who dislike tables or charts, then don't use them. There is no rule that says you have to make a table or a chart to present your findings—you could present them in a paragraph if that is what works best for you. That said, it has been our experience that even the most numbers-averse of faculty find that a well-organized table or chart provides easy-to-grasp insights into student learning.

We want to introduce you to using Excel to format the data you just summarized into easy-to-read tables and charts. A side benefit of making tables and charts in Excel is that they can be easily copied and pasted into other Microsoft Office software, like Word or PowerPoint, which can make it simple to generate a shareable report.

Formatted Tables

Tables that you might find useful include tables of your frequencies or percentages, or tables showing the averages and standard deviations for each of your data elements. To create a formatted table, you will need to set up a space in your spreadsheet that has clear column and row labels to indicate what is in the cells of the table, just like we described for frequencies and percentages tables. In fact, if you are following along in Excel we encourage you to format your existing frequencies table.

Click on any cell in your table, then go to the Insert tab and click Table. This will result in Excel selecting your table and asking you to verify its selection. The question it specifically asks is "Where is the data for your table?" If Excel has made a mistake in selecting your table, you can use your mouse to select the correct cells. You'll also see a check box below this verification asking if your table has headers. Headers are the labels for your columns, so you should leave this box checked. When you click OK, your selected cells will convert into a formatted table.

You can alter the appearance of your table using options in the Design tab, which should be the active tab if you click on any cell in your formatted table. We encourage you to play around with various styles and style options until you find the appearance that works best for you.

Stacked Bar Charts

A stacked bar chart is used to display either frequencies or percentages of each possible score for each component in your data set. These charts make it easy to see the distribution of student performance. As with tables, it is generally easier for people to understand a stacked bar chart when it is used to present percentages.

To create a stacked bar chart, you need to create a frequencies or percentages table, as described previously. Click on any cell in the table, then click the Insert tab, and then tell it what type of chart to insert. In this case, you want a 100% Stacked Column chart, so hover over the Column options until you see the correct name appear and then click the icon to create the chart. If you are following along, try this with your percentages table.

You can click and drag the chart to any location in your spreadsheet. If you click on your chart, you should see the Design tab above. Within the Design tab you can explore the many options for the look of your chart, and we encourage you to try them out to find the design that works best for you and your colleagues. We chose to edit the title and include data labels to show the percentage values, as shown in Figure 10.1.

Figure 10.1. A stacked bar chart showing the percentages of students who earned each possible score on each component of the written communication rubric.

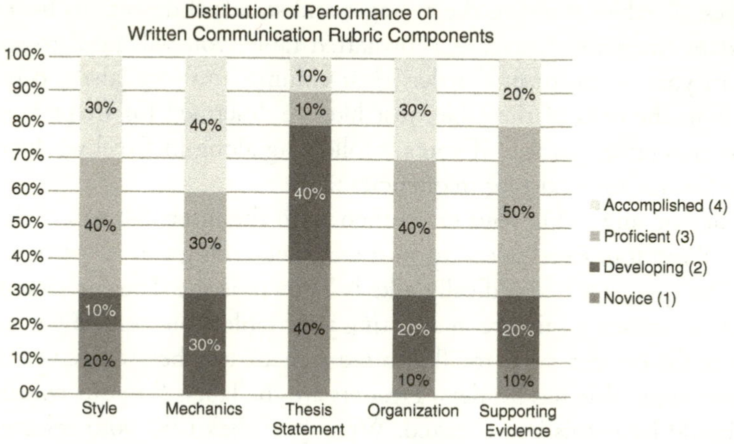

Rubric Data

The examples we've used throughout this module show us working with rubric data, so hopefully you have a sense of how you might work with your rubric data. Just to be clear, let's look at how we set up a spreadsheet for rubric data and the most useful ways to summarize and present that data.

When setting up your Excel spreadsheet for your rubric data, you'll want to make your first column student names or codes, and then make each subsequent column represent a component of your rubric. Each student will be assigned a single row, with his or her scores filling in the cells of your spreadsheet, as was shown in Table 10.1.

A summary of rubric data must be produced for each component of your rubric. The two most common ways of summarizing each rubric component include either calculating an average and standard deviation for each component, or calculating an average and the percentage of students that scored at each performance level for each component of the rubric. You can use Excel to present your rubric data in a table or a chart, just like those shown in Table 10.1.

Exam Data

When setting up your Excel spreadsheet for your exam data, you'll want to make your first column student names or codes, and then make each subsequent column represent a closed-ended item on your exam. Each student will be assigned a single row. In the cells of your spreadsheet you will want to indicate whether or not each student answered each item correctly. To do this you enter a 1 if a student was correct and a 0 if a student was incorrect. For each item, you then sum up the number of students who got the answer correct.

To present your closed-ended exam item data, you might choose to present a table showing the number of students who got each item correct, or you might calculate and show the percentage of students who got each item correct.

If you have open-ended exam items that you have scored with a rubric, please follow the instructions for rubric data discussed previously.

Survey Data

The setup of your Excel spreadsheet for your survey data, and the ways that you summarize and present your data, will differ somewhat based on the types of items you have asked. If you have survey items that allow your students to provide only a single response, such as on a response-scale item or a multiple-choice item, then your spreadsheet will be set up so that each column represents an item and each row represents a student. In the cells of your spreadsheet you will enter the response that each student gave. For response-scale items you will enter the numerical value assigned to each response, such as a 1 for Strongly Disagree, a 2 for Disagree, a 3 for Neither Agree nor Disagree, a 4 for Agree, and a 5 for Strongly Agree. This will allow you to compute an average score and standard deviation on that item. Alternatively, you can determine the frequency or percentage of the time each response was given. You can present this information in a table or a stacked bar chart.

For multiple-choice items that limited your students to one choice, you will want to enter that choice in the cells. You can either write the text of the response in the cells or assign each response a letter value, such as A = 0 times per week, B = 1 to 3 times per week, and so on, to enter into each cell. This will allow you to count the frequency of each response and calculate the percentages of responses if you like. You can present this information in a table or using stacked bar charts.

If students were allowed to pick as many responses as they like for a multiple-choice item, then you will want to set up your spreadsheet so that each possible response has its own column. If a student provided a particular response, then you will enter a 1. This will allow you to sum each column to determine how often each response was given. You can present this information in a table showing the total number of students who gave each response.

For open-ended survey items that you have coded, as described in module 9, you will want to sum how many times each code occurred, and present this information in a table. This will help you to understand which types of responses were most common.

Summary

We hope that this introduction to using Excel for assessment will help you to confidently make sense of all the scores you've generated as part of your assessment process. By completing the steps presented in this module, you'll be able to present your colleagues with meaningful summaries of the data. Those summaries will help you work together to make informed decisions about student learning and decide what actions to take to improve. The process of deciding what the data tell you, and what to do about it, is called closing the loop and is described in module 11.

CLOSING THE LOOP

Interpreting Results and Taking Action

Okay, so you've collected some evidence of student learning. You've summarized it in a way that will make sense to your colleagues. Now it's time to figure out what it's telling you and what to do about it. This step is known in assessment parlance as "closing the loop." This is the point in the assessment process where you gather together all that you've done so far and work together as a program faculty to understand student learning in your program and then use that understanding to guide actions for improvement.

While every step in the assessment cycle is important, this final step of closing the loop is what ultimately makes your assessment process a success. After all, *assessment* is, by definition, a process for understanding and improving student learning. As you engage your colleagues in the final step it may help to remind them of the purpose of assessment. Too often we have worked with programs that have done every step in the assessment process except to close the loop. When we dig deep to try to understand why the assessment process was not completed, we often find that the faculty are afraid of failure. They fear that they will find out that their students are not perfectly achieving the program's student learning outcomes and that this will make the faculty look bad. We have found that this fear can be overcome with patience and a clear, consistent message that faculty do not look bad when students do not learn perfectly, but we do look bad if we never try to be better.

In this module we guide you through a step-by-step process for closing the loop. These steps include organizing, presenting, interpreting, recommending, and taking action.

Step 1: Get Organized

More than likely you've been working on the assessment of this outcome for multiple academic terms, and it's possible that multiple people have been involved in the process. For most faculty this means that the first thing you need to do in order to close the loop is to gather together all of the relevant materials. This is analogous to assembling your *mise en place* in cooking; it sets you up for an effective and efficient process. In particular, assemble the following things for the outcome that you are working to close the loop on:

- The student learning outcome you are focusing on. Having the exact wording of the outcome at your fingertips can be helpful when discussing the evidence and deciding what it means and how to act on it.
- Your curriculum map and—if you made one for the outcome you are focusing on—your outcome map. Maps are essential for understanding how students achieved the learning they have demonstrated and are useful for determining where to make changes for improvement. For more on maps, see module 4, "Curriculum and Outcome Mapping: Understanding the Path to Student Learning in Your Program."
- The assessment measurement tools themselves (e.g., the scoring rubric, exam items, survey items). If you are looking at student work with a rubric, it can be helpful to gather both the rubric and the assignment instructions. Knowing what students were asked to do can enrich your discussion of what they are demonstrating.
- Your assessment data. This includes things like the rubric scores, exam item scores, and survey item responses that you have analyzed and described in a way that your faculty should be comfortable with. You can find ideas and instructions for how to use Microsoft Excel to do this in module 10, "Organizing, Summarizing, and Presenting Your Evidence: Using Microsoft Excel to Make Sense of Your Data."

Your primary purpose in getting these things together is to facilitate discussion. A bonus of this prep work is that it will be easy to update your assessment record with these documents. For more on what goes into your assessment record check out module 12, "Record Keeping: Keeping Track of Your Work."

Step 2: Present the Process and Results

A clear presentation of assessment results begins with a summary of the process by which you obtained those results. Hopefully, you've been able to keep your colleagues informed about and involved in the assessment process throughout, so this presentation should serve as a reminder of what's been going on. If you'll be presenting information about more than one of your outcomes, you'll want to organize your presentation by outcome, presenting them one at a time.

The most important principle to follow when presenting your results, and later when deciding what they mean and what to do about them, is to involve as many people in the process as possible. Ideally, all of the program faculty will be involved. For example, you might dedicate an entire program faculty meeting to this topic, or set aside a large block of time at a program retreat. If only one person, or a small number of people, understand the process that was followed and have a chance to review the results or decide how to interpret the results, then the rest of the faculty will be less likely to act on any recommendations that stem from that interpretation.

You should begin your presentation with the full text of the learning outcome and then walk your colleagues through your process. Explain what evidence you chose to examine and why, including what course(s) and students that evidence came from, who was involved in developing the assessment measures, what those measures look like, and who was involved in applying the assessment measurement tools. Once everyone is clear on the process that has been followed, it is time to look at the results.

If you have employed more than one assessment measurement tool, such as a rubric and items on a survey, then for each outcome you will want to organize your results by the tool they have come from. For example, let's say a theological studies program faculty used a rubric and survey items in the assessment of their ethical reasoning outcome. To clearly present the results by outcome, they have chosen to use a stacked bar chart to present the rubric data, and then below this present the average response on each survey item. The presentation of their findings would look like Figure 11.1.

As discussed in module 10, "Organizing, Summarizing, and Presenting Your Evidence: Using Microsoft Excel to Make Sense of Your Data," there is no one correct way to present your results. The approach you select needs to make sense to your colleagues. So, if you are a group of faculty who loves statistics and tables filled with numbers, then that is how you should share your findings. If you like visual displays, such as stacked bar charts, then that is how you should share the findings. If you are most comfortable with descriptive sentences, then go for it. If you are uncertain about the best way to display your findings, module 10 presents the most effective ways to share data for each of the three assessment measurement tools we have presented in this book: rubrics (module 7), exams (module 8), and surveys (module 9).

Step 3: Interpret the Results

Once everyone understands the assessment process that has been followed and has seen the results, it's time to work together to decide what your results mean. When discussing the results, you will try to answer the question of whether the level of student learning meets your expectations; in other words, you have to ask yourself if the demonstrated learning is "good enough." There are two basic approaches to answering this question.

The first approach is to evaluate your results in relation to a criterion for success. Essentially, this is an absolute standard that establishes a minimum acceptable level of performance. Ideally, the criterion is established at the beginning of the assessment process, when you are designing your measurement tool. It is decided entirely by you and your colleagues and is based on what you would hope to see in terms of student performance. When you have assessment measurement tools that were developed in-house, the setting of a criterion is usually the best approach to determining success. It's important to understand that the criterion you set is not a hard-and-fast rule. It is more like a good starting point for discussion. For example, let's say that the criterion for success on the ethical reasoning rubric scores (shared in Figure 11.1) was the expectation that at least 70% of the students would demonstrate learning consistent with the Above Average or Excellent levels of the rubric. In this situation students fell below that criterion on both ethical issue identification (with 61.11% hitting the mark) and application of ethical perspective (with 66.67% hitting the mark). Students just passed the mark on evaluation of different perspectives, with around 72.23% in the top half of the rubric. Even though students hit the mark on their ability to evaluate different perspectives, the faculty might still decide that performance could be better and proceed with actions for improvement of that component.

The second approach you can take is to compare your students' results to those of another group of students. For example, if you administered a national survey you might compare the mean responses of your students to those of students at similar institutions and decide that your students' scores are "good enough" if they are equal to or greater than those of the comparator group. Or, if you prefer, you could compare the frequencies of certain responses, rather than looking at means. Using a comparison approach makes sense when your results are from measures for which it is unclear what an absolute standard might be, such as a survey. One challenge to this approach is that it assumes you have an appropriate comparator group, something that is not always available for in-house assessment measurement tools.

Figure 11.1. Findings from the rubric and survey used to assess a theological studies program's ethical reasoning outcome.

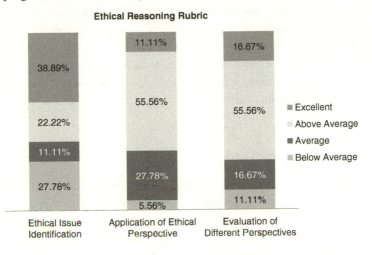

Survey items

Items	Average Response
Please indicate your ability to:	5 = Excellent, 4 = Very good, 3 = Good, 2 = Fair, 1 = Poor
Apply the ethical guidelines of your discipline when making decisions	3.59
Use the ethical guidelines of your discipline to evaluate new or different points of view on a topic	3.12

One way that you can establish a comparator group for in-house assessment measurement tools is to make a comparison between students in your program, such as between graduating senior students and first-year students. This would help you understand how much your curriculum has contributed to growth in the relevant knowledge, skill, or value. Making this type of comparison requires that you have an idea of how much growth is "good enough." You could apply a statistical test to see whether the difference is significant (i.e., not due to chance), but a statistically significant difference is not the same thing as a meaningful difference, so you will still have to apply some subjective judgment.

The question of significance is related to another issue that sometimes arises when faculty are interpreting assessment results, namely, questions about methodology, or the reliability or validity of your data. That is, faculty sometimes question whether they can believe the data. For some faculty these questions stem from their methodological expertise. For example, to faculty in the social sciences, assessment studies sometimes seem unscientific compared to their own research. In this situation it sometimes helps to talk about assessment as applied research. For those faculty who are resistant to the findings because they worry that they might be interpreted as suggesting that faculty are doing something wrong, it can help to describe less-than-desirable results as "areas of opportunity."

Step 4: Make Recommendations

If you have decided that your results suggest that students are achieving each of the identified components of a given learning outcome at a satisfactory level, then you may not feel the need to recommend any changes to the curriculum or pedagogy of your program. However, given that there is always room for improvement, you may want to raise the bar moving forward by increasing your criterion for success. Another time you might not want to make changes to your program is when you feel the assessment process did not provide a clear picture. For example, you might determine that the assessment measurement tool did not quite get at the right components of your outcome, or you might feel too few students were included in the process for any decisions to be made. In this type of situation, the decisions you make might be to revise or repeat your process before you make any changes to your curriculum for improvement. While it can be frustrating to complete an assessment cycle and reach this conclusion, please know that it is an accepted type of assessment decision. The experience of making this type of decision will likely improve the way that you design and carry out future assessment cycles so that this kind of decision does not have to happen often.

However, if you decided that there is room for improvement on any component of the learning outcome, then you will need to figure out the best course of action for achieving the desired improvement. In this case, the first thing you'll need to do is refer back to your curriculum or outcome map to see where in the curriculum that outcome is addressed, as well as how it is addressed (by what method and at what level). In particular, you want to look for any gaps, in either the curriculum or the pedagogy.

For example, if the results of an assessment exam in a psychology program showed that only 65% of senior psychology majors demonstrated an acceptable level of ability to select an appropriate methodology for a research question, you would look at which courses addressed this skill and how the skill was addressed. Looking back to the curriculum map for our hypothetical psychology program (presented as Table 4.2 in module 4, "Curriculum and Outcome Mapping: Understanding the Path to Student Learning in Your Program," we can see that this skill is introduced in the Psychology Research Methods course (Psy 201) but is not explicitly addressed again until the Senior Thesis course (Psy 490), where the skill is expected to be mastered. In other words, nowhere in the curriculum is there an intentional opportunity for students to practice, or develop, this skill before they need to use it at an expert level for their thesis. The pattern of instruction in our example psychology program provides a possible explanation for why students' learning was not at an acceptable level and points to some possibilities for actions to take to improve student learning on this outcome. In particular, the pattern suggests that there are opportunities in the curriculum between the research methods course and the thesis course to add or change something.

Outcome maps can be particularly helpful in understanding why your students did or did not achieve a given learning outcome. By specifying not only where and at what level but also details about how an outcome is addressed, an outcome map provides rich information about students' learning experiences in the program that could suggest methods for improving student learning. For example, let's say our theological studies faculty decide that their assessment results indicate that their students are not successfully achieving any of the components of their ethical reasoning outcome, but their curriculum map shows that ethical reasoning is covered in most courses. Here is where an outcome map is particularly helpful. It might show that, although ethical reasoning is covered several times, the topic is addressed primarily through readings and lectures without any accompanying discussions, activities, or assignments.

The next step is to decide what actions to recommend that will lead to improvement. There are several types of recommendations you might make. You could recommend changes to the curriculum, for example, by adding a course or changing the sequence of courses. The former might be appropriate if a learning outcome is not currently being addressed in the curriculum, while the latter might be appropriate if the learning outcome is addressed, but at the wrong point in the curriculum. Another type of recommendation is to change the pedagogy in certain courses, for example, by adding class time devoted to a topic, increasing the number of or changing the type of assignments related to the topic, or adding certain activities that you think would enhance learning. A final type of recommendation is to allocate additional resources to support a particular type of learning. For example, if students' writing skills need improvement you might decide to invest in writing tutors who could help students with their writing assignments.

In selecting which type of actions to recommend, we suggest that you start small. That is, think about small changes you might make to what you're already doing rather than making dramatic changes, such as adding a brand-new course to your curriculum. For example, our theological studies faculty might choose to incorporate activities and assignments that require students to apply ethical reasoning skills in existing courses, rather than adding a course that focuses on developing this skill set.

It is also important to be specific and concrete in your recommendations. That is, phrase your recommendations in terms of actions rather than goals. For example, "Improve student writing" as a recommendation is not very helpful, but "Increase the number of writing assignments in required sophomore- and junior-level courses" is helpful. Even more helpful would be to specify what types of writing assignments will be added to which courses.

Step 5: Implement and Document Recommended Actions

The next step is to actually implement your recommended actions. In order to do so, you need to decide on a timeline and assign responsibility for each action. The documentation does not have to be complex. It can be a simple table that captures what each recommendation is, the actions to be taken, the timeline for when actions are supposed to occur, and the name of the faculty member who will be responsible for following through.

For example, let's say the faculty in a civil engineering program have examined their students' ability to communicate effectively in writing and decided that multiple actions are needed to improve student writing. They have decided that students clearly need more writing experiences, that incorporating peer review will have a positive impact on final papers, and that agreeing on a common writing style will make instruction more consistent and coherent across the curriculum, which they believe will result in better student writing. The documentation of these recommendations looks like Table 11.1.

TABLE 11.1

Example Table Documenting Implementation of Recommendations

Recommendation	Action to Be Taken	Date	Lead
Document with grades the importance of clear and effective writing by adding essay questions to exams in all required courses.	Add essay questions to junior level engineering exams.	Fall 2017	T. Smith
Select common writing style guidelines and make them available to faculty and students.	Select a writing handbook.	Spring 2018	N. Moore
	Require students in the first-year project course to purchase the handbook.	Fall 2018	
Add peer review of drafts of papers to the first-year and senior project courses.	Conduct peer reviews of the guidelines.	Fall 2017	O. Rodriguez
	Implement the guidelines.	Spring 2018	

This action plan should be added to the program's assessment record and updated as needed when each action is completed.

Summary

Closing the loop means that you have figured out what your assessment results mean and taken action on those results in order to improve student learning. It involves organizing and presenting your results; deciding what those results tell you about student learning; developing specific, concrete recommendations for changes that you believe will lead to improvements in student learning; implementing the recommendations; and documenting the actions taken.

12

RECORD KEEPING

Keeping Track of Your Work

Having a record of what you've done for each outcome as you've assessed it is important for keeping the ongoing work of assessment meaningful, manageable, and sustainable. As you'll recall from module 1, "An Overview of Assessment Concepts and Principles: Improving Student Learning," assessment is an ongoing and cyclical process. As we discussed in module 5, "Planning: Creating a Meaningful and Manageable Assessment Plan for Your Program," you assess one or two of your program's student learning outcomes at a time, and after you move through all of them, you come back to reassess each. Your record will serve as a road map for how to approach the assessment of each outcome as it comes back around, remind you of changes you made so that you can determine if they were effective, and provide essential information for reports needed during program review and accreditation. In this module we'll provide a guide for what to include in your assessment record, as well as a few tips for storing your record and organizing all that is in it.

What to Keep in Your Record

There are two broad categories of artifacts to keep in your record. The first category includes documents that speak to the big picture. These documents will help to provide context for your assessment work. Items in this category include your

- program mission statement, student learning goals, and student learning outcomes;
- curriculum map, as well as any outcome maps you have made; and
- assessment plan.

Each of these artifacts may evolve as a natural result of the assessment process, and keeping them with the assessment record can both serve as reminder that these are things that naturally evolve as a result of assessment and make it easy to locate them when such a change is needed. For example, you might learn something about the nature of your program and wish to make an edit to your mission statement (as described in module 2, "Mission, Goals, and Outcomes: Looking at the Big Picture"). You might decide that the phrasing of a learning outcome you've assessed needs a change (as described in module 3, "Student Learning Outcomes: Articulating What You Want Students to Learn"). If a change for improvement that you decide on alters how a course is taught, the sequencing of courses in your curriculum, or adds or removes a course from your curriculum, then your map will need to be updated to reflect this (as described in module 4, "Curriculum and Outcome Mapping: Understanding the Path to Student Learning in Your Program"). Finally, you'll want to be sure to update your assessment plan as changes are made to it and it is added on to over time (as described in module 5, "Planning: Creating a Meaningful and Manageable Assessment Plan for Your Program").

The second category of artifacts to keep in your assessment record includes documentation of the steps you took to assess each of your student learning outcomes. On subsequent assessments of each outcome, your record will provide the benefit of perspective on what you did before, what worked and what didn't about that process, and what needs to be done now. Having a clear record of what came before will also save you time, largely because you do not have to start from scratch the next time around. For each of your student learning outcomes, you will want to include the following:

- Assessment measurement tools (exam items, rubrics, survey items, etc.)
- Data (including your Excel spreadsheet)
- Reports (if you produced these)
- Notes on the decisions you made, including actions taken for improvement

Having the assessment measurement tools you created the first time around will be a big time-saver. After all, developing an assessment measurement tool, like a rubric or set of exam items, can take a semester or sometimes longer. On subsequent assessments of each student learning outcome, your assessment plan will only need to include time for a review of these tools to make sure that they will still capture agreed-upon essential learning. For more on rubrics see module 7, "Rubrics: Creating and Using Rubrics for Program Assessment"; on exam items see module 8, "Exams: Asking Questions That Provide the Answers You Need"; and on surveys see module 9, "Surveys: Finding Out What Your Students Think." For more on data, including how to use Excel to generate tables and charts that can be used in reports, see module 10, "Organizing, Summarizing, and Presenting Your Evidence: Using Microsoft Excel to Make Sense of Your Data." For more on generating useful reports and making notes of decisions and actions taken, see module 11, "Closing the Loop: Interpreting Results and Taking Action."

Student Work

One additional artifact that you might consider including in your record are copies of student work, such as the papers to which you applied the rubric or student answers to exam items. While in most cases there is no need to keep copies, there are definitely reasons you might want to keep such work. For instance, keeping the work allows you to go back and review examples that were scored in certain ways according to your rubric or exam key. This can help you to make sure that you are applying your rubric or key consistently over time by reviewing how you scored previous examples of student work. Another reason for keeping your students' work is that you might be required to for program review or accreditation. Some program review processes and some accreditation processes require you to share all or a sample of the student work you examined for assessment. So, before you decide to keep or discard student work, we encourage you to check what you are required to keep. If you do decide to keep the work, we encourage you to consider keeping only electronic records. If you have paper copies, scan them to convert them into electronic records, and then shred and recycle the paper— or follow your institution's FERPA (Family Educational Rights and Privacy Act of 1974)–approved guidelines for discarding student work. If you are uncertain of FERPA guidelines for your institution, we recommend checking with your institution's FERPA officer. At most institutions the registrar is the FERPA officer.

Storing Your Record

One of the most important tips we can give you about storing your assessment record is that it needs to be kept in a place where all of your program faculty colleagues can access it, such as on a shared network or cloud storage drive. Too often we've worked with programs that have had their assessment plans seriously disrupted because their record was kept on one faculty member's computer or personal drive, and that person was on sabbatical, abroad, or for some other reason not able to access the files. If you are concerned that giving everyone access could result in difficulty managing those files, such as files being accidentally edited or deleted, then consider giving different levels of permission to your colleagues. For example, your program chair, your assessment committee chair, and the lead faculty member for each outcome might need the ability to edit the files while everyone else may need only the ability to read those files. If you are uncertain about how to give different levels of permission, your institution's IT staff should be able to help you with this.

You will want to make sure that your record is located in a space that is regularly backed up. If you are using an institution-supported network drive, then most likely your IT department does that backup for you. If you are at all uncertain about whether your record will be backed up, check with IT. If they do not regularly back up the institution's drives then they may have other good solutions for you, such as storing a backup copy in a second separate location.

A final thing to consider in storing your record is that if it will include any personal student information, such as student ID numbers, then you will want to make sure that you are following your institution's guidelines for the storage of FERPA-protected information. In most cases the things that you keep in your assessment record will not require any special protections, but if you are at all uncertain, then we encourage you to reach out to your institution's FERPA officer.

Assessment Management Systems

Some institutions use assessment management systems (AMSs) that are able to to store all of the components of your assessment record. Such systems tend to do much more than just store your record. For example, they can typically be used to generate a curriculum map, provide formatting and examples for rubrics, allow you to distribute a survey online through the system, allow you to enter your rubric or exam item scores, and even help to summarize your assessment data. While some institutions have built their own custom AMSs, there are several commercially available AMSs, including such systems as LiveText, Weave, Taskstream, Tk20, and TracDat. While an AMS can do a lot for you, it is important to keep in mind that an AMS is simply a tool to assist you as you plan and carry out assessment of your program learning outcomes; the AMS does not carry out the assessment process for you. If you are uncertain if your institution has such a system, we encourage you to check with your assessment office or IT staff.

Organizing Your Record

As a number of things will be kept in your assessment records, organization is key for ease of location both by yourself and by your colleagues who will need to access the information. We recommend a fairly simple folder structure within an electronic folder for your assessment record. You'll want to begin with one clearly named folder to house your entire record; something like "Program Assessment" will work. Within this folder you'll want to have four folders: one for each of the big-picture documents and one for your student learning outcomes assessment. Within your student learning outcomes assessment folder, you'll want a folder for each of your program's learning outcomes. This structure might look something like the one shown in Figure 12.1.

Within the folders for the big-picture artifacts (i.e., mission, maps, and plan) you'll want to keep the most current version of each artifact as well as previous versions. Each version should be dated so that the most current is clear. Keeping the older versions will allow you to review the history of these artifacts, which can be very helpful in reporting during program review or accreditation processes. The history can also be helpful as you consider new edits.

Within the folder for each of your learning outcomes, it can help to make a folder for each time that the outcome is assessed. Within the folder for each cycle you will keep a copy of the second category of artifacts previously listed,

Figure 12.1. Example electronic folder organization for your program's assessment record.

- Program Assessment
  - Mission, Goals, and Outcomes
  - Curriculum and Outcome Maps
  - Assessment Plan
  - Student Learning Outcome Assessment
    - Written Communication
    - Oral Communication
    - Critical Thinking
    - Research Methodology
    - Ethical Reasoning
    - Disciplinary Knowledge

including your assessment measurement tool, such as your rubric or exam items and key; your Excel spreadsheet of data; any reports you generated; and notes on decisions made and actions for improvement. This way, each time you go to assess each outcome you will have all of the relevant information at your fingertips.

Summary

It is important to keep a clear and detailed record of your program's assessment of your student learning outcomes. Your record should include not only "big-picture" items, like your mission statement, curriculum map, and assessment plan, but also the specific details of your assessment process for each of your program's student learning outcomes. You'll find that keeping everything related to your assessment plan together, and in a shared location that is accessible by all members of your program, will have benefits. Such benefits include reducing your workload on subsequent assessments of each of your learning outcomes and having the details you'll need for academic program review and accreditation processes.

13

CREATING A CULTURE OF ASSESSMENT

Tips for Keeping Assessment Meaningful, Manageable, and Sustainable

Our combined experience in assessment has taught us that the assessment process in the real world is often messy and that despite the best efforts of faculty the process often stalls. Our experiences have also allowed us insight into how to keep the assessment process moving successfully in your program.

First, beyond just keeping assessment moving along, we want to make sure you understand what it is that we mean by successful assessment. Our definition of *success* is derived from the definition of *assessment* that we first presented in module 1. Our definition of *assessment* stresses that it is a systematic process that is used to understand and improve student learning. The emphasis in this definition is on understanding and improving student learning. This suggests that the process should be meaningful and impactful. Our *assessment* definition also notes that it is a systematic process, which suggests that assessment should be considered an essential part of the ongoing work of your program. In addition, because assessment is done by faculty, it should be conducted in such a way that it fits within the workload of faculty in your program. In other words, successful assessment is meaningful, manageable, and sustainable.

Throughout this book we have shared tips designed to help you avoid some of the mistakes that can lead to inaction or assessment burnout and ensure your assessment efforts are successful. In this module we have compiled and expanded on those tips and ideas for ease of reference.

Leadership

Whether your program assessment will be led by a single person or by a committee, assigning leadership for assessment will help to ensure that your assessment plans are carried out and sustained over time. Ideally, the person leading assessment in your program will be someone other than the program chair. While it is important that your chair be involved and supportive, encouraging faculty other than the chair to take responsibility for assessment can potentially lead to greater faculty ownership of and engagement in the assessment process, as well as help to sustain assessment activity through leadership changes in the program.

Equally important is the clear support of senior leadership at your institution. Although it's never a good idea for assessment to be a top-down proposition, clear messaging by a dean or provost about the value of assessment is critical. Those messages are most effective when they are embedded in a communication about a broader topic, such as "academic excellence." Academic leaders can also be helpful through providing recognition and material support for assessment work. Specific tips for administrators and other academic leaders about providing such recognition and support are presented later in this module.

Engage the Faculty

While it is important that a person or committee be charged with leading assessment, it is essential that as many of your program faculty as possible are engaged in the process. Not every faculty member needs to be involved in every step of the assessment process, but the work will be richer for sharing responsibilities for assessment. Bringing multiple perspectives and experiences into all steps in the process will result in assessment that better reflects the interests and needs of your program faculty. In addition, through the process of collaborating, faculty colleagues develop a better understanding of exactly what and how students are learning in your program, which can enrich pedagogical practices and course content choices of those faculty. Finally, when you are engaged in the process of assessment, you tend to develop a sense of ownership of the process, which leads to greater interest in the findings and commitment to making changes for improvement.

One of the easiest ways to engage faculty in the assessment process is through discussion, in either program faculty meetings or retreats. For example, you might devote one or two program faculty meetings each term to focusing on some aspect of assessment. One of those meetings might be used to develop or refine the program's learning goals and outcomes, while the other might be used to review and discuss the most recent assessment results. Retreats can also be a good venue for in-depth discussions about assessment. For example, you might set aside two hours at an end-of-year retreat to review and discuss all of the assessment evidence that was gathered throughout the year. However, it is still important to regularly include assessment on program faculty meeting agendas so you make it clear that assessment is a normal part of the business of the program. In most meetings this agenda item can be a brief update on steps taken in the current assessment plan.

It can also be helpful to assign small groups of faculty to work on specific components of the assessment process, such as developing an assessment measurement tool (e.g., an exam or a rubric), creating a curriculum map, applying a rubric to student work, or analyzing assessment data and putting together a presentation or short report of the findings.

Make It Meaningful

One source of faculty resistance to assessment is the perception that it is administrative busywork; for example, we've even heard assessment referred to as "administrivia." In other words, it feels like a lot of work without much benefit. The external pressures described in the introduction to this book do not help dispel this perception. Thus, it is important to find ways of making assessment meaningful and beneficial.

One of the most important things you can do toward that end is to focus on what faculty care about. At a general level, what most faculty care about is student learning, so it's helpful to focus on assessment as a process for understanding and improving student learning. More specifically, there may be particular aspects of your program that faculty are passionate about. For example, perhaps your faculty are proud of the fact that your program requires a community-based learning experience that emphasizes understanding the structural causes of homelessness. Start there. Perhaps you can develop a rubric to apply to the reflection papers that students write in their community-based learning course.

Another aspect of assessment that can resonate with faculty is an emphasis on improvement. As educators (as human beings really), there is always room to grow and to be better at what we do. Assessment will help you to strengthen and improve what you do as an educator in order to improve what and how well your students learn. As student learning is a primary goal of your program, keeping your focus on improving student learning can serve as a powerful motivator to engage in and sustain assessment activities.

Start Small and Keep It Simple

One of the biggest mistakes we've observed is trying to do too much too soon. It can be difficult to get assessment going, or keep it moving, if you feel as if you have to assess every outcome all of the time. Feeling as if you have to do everything at once often results in doing nothing at all. It is a best practice in assessment to focus on only one or two outcomes at a time and to allow yourself one or two years to complete the assessment process for each outcome. Developing and documenting an assessment plan that follows this approach will help to keep assessment going in meaningful, manageable, and sustainable ways.

Another mistake that we have seen too often is the use of complex or time-consuming methodologies when a much simpler method would get the job done. For example, conducting senior exit interviews with every graduating senior in your program will take a great deal of time to complete, and even more time to transcribe what was said and then analyze those responses. This approach might result in a great deal of incredibly rich evidence, but the time commitment is likely more than most faculty will find manageable. When assessment requires more work than is feasible given other commitments, it will most likely not get done. Choosing a simpler, more manageable alternative, like a senior exit survey, will still result in useful evidence and be less likely to stall your assessment efforts.

Build on Existing Practices and Resources

Although many faculty might think they need to start from scratch with assessment, that is rarely the case. More often than not, there are practices in place in your program that, with minor modifications, can provide evidence of student learning. For example, your program might have a senior capstone project. If so, you're very close to having evidence of student learning. The only missing piece is a systematic analysis of student performance on those projects with a rubric. Or, perhaps you already do exit surveys with your seniors to gauge student satisfaction with the program. With a few modifications, consistent with the principles outlined in module 9, "Surveys: Finding Out What Your Students Think," you can use the survey as an indirect measure of student learning. In each case, the approach has the advantage of requiring very little additional work beyond what you have already been doing.

In addition to existing practices within your program, there are very likely existing resources you can tap into in your discipline or from a higher education organization. For example, many of the sciences, social sciences, and humanities have developed resources such as learning outcomes for the discipline, rubrics to assess specific learning outcomes, and other methodologies. In addition, many disciplinary accrediting agencies have articulated learning outcomes for the programs they accredit and offer workshops, publications, or other resources designed to help faculty with the assessment process. You can also download assessment rubrics for key learning outcomes on the AAC&U website. Referred to as "VALUE rubrics," these 16 rubrics represent such learning outcomes as critical thinking, quantitative literacy, information literacy, written communication, global learning, and civic engagement, among others (Rhodes, 2010). The rubrics were designed to be neutral in regard to discipline or context of the student work, with the intent that you will refine them to be appropriate to your specific context. There is still work in refining an existing rubric, but at least you won't have to start from scratch.

In addition, there may be institutional resources your program could take advantage of. For example, your campus may have an assessment office that provides resources to support program assessment. Those resources might include consulting support for writing learning outcomes or creating surveys, workshops about different assessment measures, sample rubrics, or templates for assessment reports. If your institution does not have an assessment office, then the institutional research office might be able to provide assistance in some areas, such as survey design and administration.

Use Methods With Which People Are Comfortable

One source of faculty resistance to assessment is how "social science-y" it seems, since they tend to envision tests and surveys and statistics. However, as was noted in module 6, "Assessment Measurement Tools: Determining What Your Students Are Learning," there is more than one way to measure achievement of a given outcome. Thus, we suggest that you select methods with which your colleagues feel more comfortable, and those tend to be methods that are similar to approaches or research methods used in your discipline. For example, faculty in the arts are used to evaluating artistic works, so spelling out the evaluation criteria in a rubric designed to assess key elements in students' artistic work might be appropriate. Similarly, historians are used to working with narratives, so they might be more comfortable having students write a reflective essay on their learning experiences, using guiding prompts, rather than administering a survey.

Have a Written Plan

An assessment plan lays out who does what when. It shows you what needs to be done now, what can be completed later, and how to stay on track to assess one or two student learning outcomes each year. Assessment plans also specify who is responsible for completing each step in the process. A written plan is instrumental in conducting meaningful, manageable, and sustainable assessment of your program's student learning outcomes.

For a detailed description of what goes into an assessment plan, check out module 5, "Planning: Creating a Meaningful and Manageable Assessment Plan for Your Program."

Be Flexible

Having a clear, written assessment plan is important; however, as the saying goes, "The best-laid plans of mice and men often go awry." Assessment work is done in the real world, and we don't always have the luxury of being able to follow a plan that begins at Step 1. For example, perhaps you already have some assessment evidence that was collected before you clarified your learning outcomes. Or perhaps you realize after the fact that you have used a less-than-ideal assessment measurement tool. Or your curriculum map suggests that changes should be made before you even gather any evidence. Don't panic; instead, be flexible. Sometimes the assessment process is a little messy and nonlinear, but you can adapt. It's okay to start where you are. It's okay to revise your outcomes or your curriculum before you've even collected assessment data. It's okay to revise your methods if they yield results that aren't meaningful.

Keep a Record

Maintaining a record of your assessment work has multiple benefits. A major benefit of your record is that it keeps you from having to reinvent the wheel every time you cycle back to reassess an outcome. This can be especially useful when there has been a leadership transition in your program and no one remembers exactly what was done before. Another benefit is that your record will help you determine the cause of any improvements in student learning, since you will have kept track of what changes were made.

Your record will tell you what you did; show you the assessment measurement tools you used, such as your rubric; and remind you of what decisions you made about student learning and actions for improvement. Having that information readily available can help streamline your ongoing assessment process.

For a list of things to keep in your record and suggestions for how to store it, check out module 12, "Record Keeping: Keeping Track of Your Work."

A Few Tips for Those in Academic Leadership Roles

While the primary focus of this book is on conducting program assessment, academic administrators and other academic leaders can provide key support for increasing faculty engagement in and commitment to program assessment. Here we provide just a few tips for institution-wide approaches to increasing successful program assessment.

Recognize and Support Program Assessment Work

Throughout this book we've provided tips for making assessment manageable and sustainable. However, there's no getting around the fact that, however streamlined an assessment plan is, assessment still requires that faculty complete the work. It may be very little additional work, but faculty are already feeling stretched by what seems to be an ever-increasing set of demands placed on them. To address this issue, it's important that assessment work be recognized and supported in a material way. It doesn't take much. For example, on our campus we offer small assessment grants for assessment projects that can be completed during the summer. Successful grant projects have included things like applying a rubric to a sample of student work that was collected during the academic year or developing an exam that will assess multiple outcomes and be given in a program's senior capstone course. To recognize faculty assessment work, you might post short descriptions of successful assessment projects (e.g., creating a new rubric or successfully "closing the loop") on a website called "Celebrating Assessment" or "Assessment Success Stories." This approach has the added benefit of enhancing the motivation of other faculty by showing that assessment is not difficult or onerous, as well as providing helpful examples that other faculty can then adapt within their own program.

A more substantial investment that administrators can make to support faculty is to have a person or office that is charged with providing professional assistance to faculty in their assessment work. Such a person does not need to be a full-time administrator; in fact, we've seen successful models at smaller institutions in which a tenured faculty member is given reassigned time to take on this role. One advantage of this approach is that the person has considerable credibility with faculty. However the position is constructed, it's important that the person is presented to the faculty as a consultant who can provide advice, expertise, and resources rather than the person who will do the assessment for them. It's also important that the person not be perceived as the "assessment police," that is, someone who checks on their assessment work.

Build Into Academic, Strategic, and Budget Planning Processes

One of the most effective ways of ensuring that assessment is sustainable is to build it into work that is already being done. Strategic planning and academic planning and review are two areas where it is easy to embed assessment, or some elements of assessment, into existing processes. For example, if a new academic program is being proposed, you can require that learning outcomes for the program, as well as a curriculum map and a multiyear assessment plan, be included in the proposal. In addition, your academic program review process could include evidence of achievement of student learning outcomes as part of the self-study.

Assessment can be embedded in strategic planning processes in similar ways. For example, if your institution has a process in which people submit formal requests for strategic funding, the request template could be modified to include a plan for assessing the effectiveness of the initiative. For initiatives that are designed to impact student learning or success, the assessment plan would include methods for assessing student learning. Then, after the initiative has been funded and implemented, you can request that results of the assessment be submitted in order to continue the funding.

Another way to link assessment to the budget planning process is to tie program-level budget allocations to assessment activity. For example, if a new faculty line becomes available, the decision about where to allocate that line might be based in part on the level and quality of assessment in a program. That is, programs that are engaged on a regular basis in meaningful assessment would have a better shot at getting the line.

Whatever the method, what is important is that you're sending a clear message that assessment of student learning is part of the work that faculty and administrators do.

Summary

Successful assessment is meaningful, manageable, and sustainable and should be considered an essential part of the ongoing work of a program. Some helpful strategies for ensuring that assessment is successful include assigning leadership, communicating the value of assessment, engaging the faculty, keeping the process simple, building on existing practices and resources, having a written plan, keeping a record of assessment activities, providing recognition and support, and embedding assessment into ongoing planning processes.

Additional Assessment Resources

We've compiled the following list of additional resources for those of you who are hungry for more assessment information and ideas. We encourage you to check out these resources, and to seek out even more on your own. A good place to start looking for additional information that may help you with your program assessment is with your professional disciplinary organization.

AAC&U's VALUE Project

Association of American Colleges & Universities. (n.d.). *VALUE*. Retrieved from www.aacu.org/value

The VALUE (Valid Assessment of Learning in Undergraduate Education) project is an assessment initiative of AAC&U as part of its Liberal Education and America's Promise (LEAP) initiative. Each of the 16 VALUE rubrics is available for download on the website. You'll also find information about AAC&U's current projects and activities.

Assessment in Creative Disciplines

Chase, D., Ferguson, J. L., & Hoey, J. J. (2014). *Assessment in creative disciplines: Quantifying and qualifying the aesthetic*. Champaign, IL: Common Ground.

This book focuses on assessment approaches, topics, and concerns that are unique to faculty in the creative disciplines. The text is rich with concrete examples and the approaches may be used to assess at the course level and at the program level.

Classroom Assessment

Angelo, T. A., & Cross, K. P. (1993). *Classroom assessment techniques: A handbook for college teachers* (2nd ed.). San Francisco, CA: Jossey-Bass.

This book is a rich source of ideas for assessing learning within individual courses. Many of the techniques may also be used to design assignments for the purpose of program assessment.

Defining a Degree

Lumina Foundation. (2016). *DQP: Degree Qualifications Profile*. Retrieved from http://degreeprofile.org

The Degree Qualifications Profile (DQP) defines a set of five broad categories of proficiencies that work together to define what degrees mean in terms of specific student learning outcomes. The DQP may be a useful instrument in thinking through what your degree means and writing learning outcomes for your program or institution.

Growing a Culture of Assessment

Maki, P. L. (Ed.). (2010). *Coming to terms with student outcomes assessment: Faculty and administrators' journeys to integrating assessment in their work and institutional culture*. Sterling, VA: Stylus.

This edited volume shares the first-person accounts of faculty and administrators who have come to terms with assessment and built a culture. A variety of programs and institutional types are represented.

Involving Students in the Assessment Process

Chappuis, J., & Stiggins, R. J. (2016). *An introduction to student-involved assessment FOR learning* (7th ed.). New York, NY: Pearson.

This text presents a model of assessment that involves students in just about every step of the process. While primarily written for K–12 educators, the principles, even many of the specific techniques, work well for faculty in higher education.

National Institute for Learning Outcomes Assessment

National Institute for Learning Outcomes Assessment. (2012). *National Institute for Learning Outcomes Assessment: Making learning outcomes usable and transparent*. Retrieved from www.learningoutcomeassessment.org

The mission of the National Institute for Learning Outcomes Assessment (NILOA) is to increase the ways that academic programs and institutions communicate and use assessment data both internally and externally. The NILOA website is filled with helpful resources and examples.

Transparency in Learning and Teaching in Higher Education Project

Winkelmes, M. (2014). *Transparency in learning and teaching in higher education.* Retrieved from www.unlv.edu/provost/teachingandlearning

Transparent teaching aims to help students understand how and why they learn content in particular ways and includes a focus on sharing learning outcomes with students. The Transparency in Learning and Teaching in Higher Education project website shares models for how to do this and research on the benefits to student learning.

Trends and Practices in Higher Education Assessment

Banta, T. W. (Ed.). (1989–). *Assessment update.* San Francisco, CA: Jossey-Bass. Retrieved from www.assessmentupdate.com

This periodical publishes articles about recent developments in assessment practice in higher education. The focus is on practical advice for faculty and administrators on conducting assessment in a variety of areas. Editor Trudy W. Banta is considered a pioneer in higher education learning outcomes assessment and has won several national awards for her work.

Actionable: When results of applying your measurement tool give you some idea about what to do with them; a property that comes from the design of the measurement tool.

Action Word of a Learning Outcome: The element of a student learning outcome that clearly describes the behavior to be observed.

Add-On Assessment: Assessment activities that occur outside of the formal curriculum. These are additional tasks that ask students to do something beyond their required course work.

Alternatives: The response options in a multiple-choice item.

Anonymous Survey: A survey for which the person conducting the survey cannot connect responses to the individuals who provided them.

Assessment: A systematic process for understanding and improving student learning.

Assessment Management System (AMS): An electronic system that assists with the storage and management of assessment information.

Assessment Plan: A document that indicates who is responsible for completing each step in the assessment process for a learning outcome and notes when each task is to be completed.

Authentic Assessment: Assessment that involves asking students to demonstrate their learning outcome–related knowledge or skills in a way that reflects the outcome and your discipline in a real way.

Average: The mean. Computed by adding all of the scores in your set and dividing by the number of scores in the set.

Closed-Ended Questions: Questions that require the respondent to select a response from a given set of options.

Closing the Loop: Using what you've learned about student learning outcome accomplishment to make changes designed to improve student learning.

Coding: The process of identifying themes or categories within open-ended survey responses.

Cognitive Load: The amount of information you are keeping track of and processing at any given time. This is a limited capacity resource.

Cognitive Overload: Occurs when you attempt to keep track of and process more information at one time than your capacity can handle. Also see *cognitive load*.

Confidential Survey: A survey for which the person conducting the survey knows who provided each response but does not reveal that information to anyone.

Constructed-Response Exam Items: Exam items that require brief responses to specific questions or open-ended prompts and include such exam item types as short answer, labeling diagrams, and fill in the blank.

Content Validity: When the content of the measurement tool is both relevant to the outcome being assessed and representative of the knowledge, skills, and values that were taught.

Convergence: When a combination of complementary measurement tools is used to understand achievement of a student learning outcome.

Curriculum Map: A method for depicting the alignment between a program's curriculum and the student learning outcomes of the program.

Data: Information, usually numerical, that can be used for analysis.

Dimension: Specific skills or components of a student learning outcome.

Direct Evidence of Student Learning: Student demonstrations of learning such as through completed work products or exams.

Double-Barreled Survey Item: A survey item that asks more than one question but allows only one response; can occur in closed-ended or open-ended survey items.

Embedded Assessment: Assessment process that involves collecting evidence of student learning that already exists, such as assignments or exams that were submitted for part of a course grade.

Essay Item: Open-ended exam item that asks students to respond to a prompt, allowing the response to be determined by the student.

Face Validity: A measurement tool that looks, on its face, like it measures the knowledge, skill, or value it is supposed to measure.

Fill-in-the-Blank Item: Constructed-response exam item that presents students with an incomplete sentence and asks them to fill in the missing word, number, or symbol.

Frequency: The number of times a specified score occurred in a data set.

Indirect Evidence of Student Learning: Students' perceptions of their learning, the educational environment that supports learning, and their self-reported learning-related behaviors.

In-House Exam: An exam developed by faculty within your program.

In-House Survey: A survey developed by faculty within your program.

Institutional Review Board (IRB): A committee that reviews research involving human participants to ensure that it is conducted in accordance with institutional and federal ethical guidelines.

Interrater Reliability: Consistency across raters. No matter who applies the measurement tool, the same score is found.

Label-a-Diagram Item: Constructed-response exam item that presents students with a diagram and asks them to label specific components.

Learning Statement of a Learning Outcome: The element of a student learning outcome that specifies the learning that will be demonstrated.

Levels Map: A curriculum map that indicates the level at which courses address each outcome, such as introduce (I), develop (D), or master (M).

Matching Item: Selected-response exam item that consists of two parallel lists of words or phrases that requires students to match items on one list with items on another list.

Measurement Error: The measurement of things you did not intend to capture with a measurement tool. All measurements of learning contain at least some degree of error.

Measurement Tool: A tool for measuring student achievement of a student learning outcome. The three basic types are rubrics, exams, and surveys.

Mission Statement: A mission statement explains why your program or institution exists and what it hopes to achieve. It articulates your program's or institution's essential nature, its values, and its work.

Multiple-Choice Exam Item: Selected-response exam item that includes a stem and a set of alternatives to choose from.

Multiple-Choice Survey Item: A survey item that asks a question and then provides a set of possible response options. Respondents may be asked to provide only one answer or to indicate all of the answers that apply.

Open-Ended Questions: Questions that invite the respondent to answer freely.

Opening Phrase of a Learning Outcome: The element of a student learning outcome that indicates who will demonstrate the learning.

Outcome Map: A map of the significant pedagogies, course content, assignments, and activities for a single outcome.

Overview Map: A curriculum map that indicates with check marks or Xs which courses address each outcome.

Parallel Forms Reliability: Consistency across forms or versions. Found when you have two or more versions of a measurement tool and no matter which version is applied the same score is found.

Performance Assessment: A form of authentic assessment that requires students to perform a learning outcome–related task.

Pilot Test: Testing your measurement tool prior to using it for assessment.

Problem-Solving Transfer: Using existing knowledge in a new situation or to evaluate new information.

Published Exam: An exam developed by a third party outside of your institution; often referred to as a *standardized exam*.

Published Survey: A survey developed by a third party outside of your institution; sometimes referred to as a *standardized survey*.

Random Error: Error in measurement that comes from unknown and unpredictable sources.

Random Sample: A subset of the population that was drawn so that each member of the sample had an equal and independent chance of being in the sample.

Reliability: Consistency. A reliable measurement tool gives you the same score each time you use it unless there has been a change in what you are measuring.

Response-Scale Survey Item: A survey item that presents a statement and asks the respondent to indicate his or her response using a scale.

Rubric: A guide for evaluating student work along identified dimensions. The dimensions are specific skills or components of the student learning outcome you are assessing. For each dimension, there are concrete descriptors for different levels of performance.

Selected-Response Exam Items: Exam items that require the test taker to select a response from a given set of options; includes such item types as multiple choice, true-false, and matching.

Short-Answer Item: Constructed-response exam item that asks students a direct question that requires them to provide a brief answer, such as a word or a sentence or two, or even draw an illustration.

Standard Deviation: The typical distance of scores from the average (or mean).

Standardized Exam: See *published exam*.

Stem: The question or incomplete statement component of a multiple-choice item.

Student Learning Goals: Broad statements that describe essential learning that graduates of your program should accomplish.

Student Learning Outcomes: Clear, concise statements that describe how students can demonstrate their mastery of program student learning goals.

Systematic Error: Error in measurement that comes from your measurement tools.

Test-Retest Reliability: Consistency over time. A measurement tool that gives you the same measurement each time you apply it.

True-False Item: Selected-response exam item that asks the test taker to indicate whether a statement is true or false.

Validity: Measuring what you intend to measure.

Allen, M. J. (2008, July 28). *Strategies for direct and indirect assessment of student learning.* Paper presented at SACS-COC Summer Institute, Orlando, FL. Retrieved from http://academics.lmu.edu/media/lmuacademics/strategicplan ningacademiceffectiveness/officeofassessment/Strategies%20for%20Direct%20 and%20Indirect%20Assesssment%20of%20Student%20Learning.pdf

American Bar Association. (2016–2017). *2016–2017 Standards and rules of procedure for approval of law schools.* Retrieved from www.americanbar.org/legaled

Anderson, L. W., & Krathwohl, D. R. (Eds.). (2001). *A taxonomy for learning, teaching, and assessing: A revision of Bloom's taxonomy of educational objectives.* New York, NY: Longman.

Angelo, T. A. (1995, November). Reassessing (and defining) assessment. *AAHEA Bulletin, 48*(3), 7.

Arum, R., & Roska, J. (2011). *Academically adrift: Limited learning on college campuses.* Chicago, IL: The University of Chicago Press.

Augsburg College. (2016). *Art.* Retrieved from http://www.augsburg.edu/art/

Baddeley, A. D., & Hitch, G. (1974). Working memory. *Psychology of Learning and Motivation, 8,* 47–89. doi:10.1016/S0079-7421(08)60452-1

Bates College. (n.d.). *Biology.* Retrieved from http://www.bates.edu/biology/biology-at-bates/mission/

Bok, D. (2006). *Our underachieving colleges: A candid look at how much students learn and why they should be learning more.* Princeton, NJ: Princeton University Press.

Clark, R. C., Nguyen, F., & Sweller, J. (2006). *Efficiency in learning: Evidence based guidelines to manage cognitive load.* San Francisco, CA: John Wiley.

Cooperative Institutional Research Program. (2016). *College senior survey.* Los Angeles, CA: Higher Education Research Institute. Retrieved from http://www.heri .ucla.edu/cssoverview.php

Creighton University. (n.d.). *Heider College of Business.* Retrieved from https:// business.creighton.edu/about

Davis, B. G. (2009). *Tools for teaching* (2nd ed.). San Francisco, CA: Jossey-Bass.

Family Educational Rights and Privacy Act of 1974, 20 U.S.C. § 1232g (1974).

Harrow, A. (1972). *A taxonomy of psychomotor domain: A guide for developing behavioral objectives.* New York, NY: David McKay.

Krathwohl, D. R., Bloom, B. S., & Masia, B. B. (1973). *Taxonomy of educational objectives, the classification of educational goals. Handbook II: Affective domain.* New York, NY: David McKay.

Linfield College. (n.d.). *Theatre and communication arts mission statement.* Retrieved from http://www.linfield.edu/tca/tca-mission.html

Mayer, R. E., & Wittrock, M. E. (1996). Problem-solving transfer. In D. C. Berliner & R. C. Calfee (Eds.), *Handbook of educational psychology* (pp. 47–62). New York, NY: Macmillan.

National Survey of Student Engagement. (2013). *A fresh look at student engagement.* Washington, DC: Author.

Rhodes, T. L. (2010). *Assessing outcomes and improving achievement: Tips and tools for using rubrics.* Washington, DC: Association of American Colleges & Universities.

Southern Oregon University. (2005, October). *Mathematics department mission statement.* Retrieved from http://www.souedu/math/mission-statement.html

Sweller, J. (1988). Cognitive load during problem solving: Effects on learning. *Cognitive Science, 12,* 257–285. doi:10.1207/s15516709cog1202_4

Tulane University. (n.d.). *Department of history learning goals and mission statement.* Retrieved from http://history.tulane.edu/web/default.asp?id=LearningGoalsAndMissionStatement

University of North Carolina Wilmington. (2013, March 2). *UNCW department of psychology—values, mission, & vision.* Retrieved from http://uncw.edu/psy/about/mission.html

U.S. Department of Education. (2006). *A test of leadership: Charting the future of U.S. higher education.* Washington, DC: Author.

WASC Senior College and University Commission. (2013). *2013 Handbook of accreditation* (Rev. ed.). Alameda, CA: Author.

Winkelmes, M. (2013, Spring). Transparency in teaching: Faculty share data and improve students' learning. *Liberal Education, 99*(2), 48–55.

Winkelmes, M., Bernacki, M., Butler, J., Zochowski, M., Golanics, J., & Weavil, K. H. (2016, Winter/Spring). A teaching intervention that increases underserved college students' success. *Peer Review, 18*(1/2), 31–36.

ABOUT THE AUTHORS

Laura J. Massa has served as the director of assessment at Loyola Marymount University (LMU) since 2008. In this role she has developed a variety of online resources to help LMU faculty conduct meaningful and manageable assessment. Massa regularly conducts workshops on assessment techniques at LMU, for the Western Association of Schools and Colleges (WASC) Senior College and University Commission, and at a variety of universities. As a result of her experiences teaching in the School of Education at LMU, she was invited to coauthor a text on assessment for teachers at Catholic high schools. Massa has experience as both a researcher and an assistant professor in psychology, specializing in assessment and improving student learning outcomes. Massa holds a doctorate in cognitive psychology with an emphasis in quantitative methods for the social sciences.

Margaret Kasimatis currently serves as vice provost for strategic planning and educational effectiveness at Loyola Marymount University. In that capacity she provides leadership in the areas of academic program planning and review, strategic planning, faculty development related to teaching effectiveness, educational effectiveness, accreditation, and continuing education. With more than 14 years of experience in academic administration, Kasimatis previously served as executive director of institutional research, assessment, and planning at California State Polytechnic University, Pomona, and director of assessment at Harvey Mudd College. In addition, Kasimatis has been actively engaged in regional accreditation processes through the WASC Senior College and University Commission (WSCUC). She served for six years as a WSCUC commissioner and in two of those years held the position of vice chair of the commission. She also serves as a WSCUC evaluator and was a member of the WSCUC Interim Report Committee and the WSCUC Program Review Task Force. She earned her PhD in social psychology and has held full-time faculty positions at Harvey Mudd College and Hope College.

INDEX